"Those of the Church Fathers who espoused universal salvation were moved to do so not only from the conviction that this was the testimony of scripture, but also from the radical notion that, when we say that God is love or call him Father, we are not just spouting pious nonsense, but are saying something both logically coherent and necessarily true. Keith Giles has no purpose in these pages but to demonstrate how right they were."

— DAVID BENTLEY HART, AUTHOR OF *THAT ALL SHALL BE SAVED*

"Citing scripture, ancient Church leaders, and contemporary biblical scholars, Keith Giles makes a compelling case against hell. What makes this book especially winsome is the accessible way Giles writes. The conversation is easy to follow and arguments compelling. This book is both an encyclopedic resource and conversation starter!"

— THOMAS JAY OORD, AUTHOR OF *GOD CAN'T: HOW TO BELIEVE IN GOD AND LOVE AFTER TRAGEDY, ABUSE, AND OTHER EVILS* AND *THE UNCONTROLLING LOVE OF GOD*

"*Jesus Undefeated* reveals an early church corpus who, through their common sense and sacred intuition, knew what we moderns seem to have so inexplicably forgotten. They corporately knew God far too well to believe Him capable of ever creating such a bone-torturing Hell...This lie needs to fry. And Keith, as a master conceptual chef, does just that in his wonderful new book which I heartily recommend."

"Keith, in a very readable fashion and conversational tone, reexamines the idea of the afterlife and demythologizes the concept of hell, all with a thorough application of the Bible, the Church Fathers, and theologians. But what I like most about his work is that it comes from a big heart motivated by love to include all. And isn't this the thrust of the gospel?"

"Keith Giles has crafted a deeply helpful and valuable gift that would have saved me years."

"Anyone who cares what the New Testament says about 'the End Times' owes it to themselves to read this insightful work."

"[Keith] draws our attention to something more captivatingly beautiful—the presence of Christ within us inviting us to participate in an adventure that is already happening."

"[Jesus's] message, once so counter-cultural, has been stifled, suffocated, and reduced to a tangled pile of knots on the floor of the American political scene. I can think of no better place for a Christian to begin sorting those out, and reclaiming a message that is still other-worldly after all these years, than with *Jesus Untangled.*"

— BENJAMIN L. COREY, AUTHOR OF *UNDILUTED: REDISCOVERING THE RADICAL MESSAGE OF JESUS*

"The best books about Jesus are the ones that are as challenging as they are inspiring and as entertaining as they are informative. Keith Giles nails it in *Jesus Untangled.* It's a book about love, and it's a love extended to all the different tribal factions that all-too-often fight for Christian supremacy at the expense of Christ's teachings."

— JOHN FUGELSANG, HOST OF "TELL ME EVERYTHING", SIRIUS XM RADIO

"Keith Giles runs with that company of Christ-followers committed to proclaiming that Jesus Christ is the Word of God, our final Authority for faith and practice...Fear not: Keith does not throw the Bible under the bus. But he will dethrone biblical literalism wherever it supplants the Lordship of the...Word of God."

— BRAD JERSAK, PHD, AUTHOR OF *A MORE CHRISTLIKE GOD*

"Keith Giles is a professional cow tipper, specializing in the sacred variety. Having toppled the sacred cow of religious nationalism in *Jesus Untangled*, he returns to the pasture in *Jesus Unbound*, where he overturns what may have become our most sacred cow

of all—biblical inerrancy—along with the golden calf of bibli-
cism that never lags far behind."

"In this book, Keith Giles presents us with the powerful example
of his own life as he has dared to live out the prophetic insights
he has discovered into the nature and mission of God's culture-
challenging community. Read and gain courage to risk following
his inspired and dynamic servant-leadership."

OTHER BOOKS IN THE JESUS UN SERIES

Available at Amazon.com

First Edition

Cover design and layout by Rafael Polendo (polendo.net)

Unless otherwise identified, all Scripture quotations in this publication are taken from the Holy Bible, New International Version®, NIV®. Copyright ©1973, 1978, 1984, 2011 by Biblica, Inc.™ Used by permission of Zondervan. All rights reserved worldwide. www.zondervan.com The "NIV" and "New International Version" are trademarks registered in the United States Patent and Trademark Office by Biblica, Inc.™

ESV Bible® (The Holy Bible, *English Standard Version*®), copyright © 2001 by Crossway Bibles, a publishing ministry of Good News Publishers. Used by permission. All rights reserved. www.crossway.org.

ISBN 978-1-938480-99-7

This volume is printed on acid free paper and meets ANSI Z39.48 standards.

Printed in the United States of America

 QUOIR

Published by Quoir
Oak Glen, California

www.quoir.com

JESUS
UNARMED
HOW THE PRINCE OF PEACE DISARMS OUR VIOLENCE

KEITH GILES

ACKNOWLEGEMENTS

Special thanks are in order for Rafael Polendo, Bram Watkins, Neale Locke, Brad Jersak, Greg Boyd, Bruxy Cavey, Brian Zahnd, Shane Claiborne, and of course my boys Dylan and David and my beautiful wife Wendy who makes everything worthwhile.

DEDICATION

To my Mom, the first woman I ever fell in love with. Thank you for showing me the power of love to change us from the inside out.

TABLE OF CONTENTS

FOREWORD

This is a book about Jesus and violence. Two subjects with absolutely zero overlap in the Bible, and almost constant overlap within the history of Christianity.

Whether you consider Jesus to have been the Divine Son of God, a highly evolved teacher and healer, a mystic philosopher and radical political dissident, a complete work of first century fiction or the original hippie, one fact can't be denied: he's one of the most revolutionary anti-violence figures in literature, spirituality and/or recorded history.

But we live in a time when Christians carry on a tradition of recreating Christ in their own image, and it turns out, their Jesus isn't the nonviolent bearer of compassion who demands we turn the other cheek. When it comes to war, torture, the death penalty or gun worship, some of Jesus' unauthorized fan clubs have historically, and conveniently, overlooked His teachings on how we're supposed to treat each other.

No baby comes out violent. It often takes years of conditioning. Sometimes it takes a village. One where violence is modeled as a solution to problems. This has allowed countless generations of Christians to read Jesus' words about love and forgiveness while also being taught that some violence is acceptable.

The easiest way to generate violence among a group of religious people is to justify any kind of bloodshed as divinely ordained by God. The most shameful element of Christian history is how it's been used to justify all manner of personal and institutionalized abuse.

For example, Columbus used Christianity as his justification for murder, rape enslavement and mutilation.

Slavery was backed up by much of American Christianity, as was the American apartheid that existed for 100 years afterwards.

Hitler said "My feelings as a Christian point me to my Lord and Savior as a fighter."

In 2005 the BBC reported that George W. Bush claimed God had told him to invade and occupy Iraq.

The media and religious leaders have, over decades, inflamed tensions to such an extent that every now and then some feverishly motivated Christians decide that God's given them a pass on the rule of law—and His own Commandments. With alarming frequency, we've seen self-proclaimed Christians turn to violence in the hopes that it would change policy.

In Illinois, Terry-Joe Sedlacek heard on Fox News that his pastor Fred Winters was in favor of Same-Sex Marriage. Mr. Sedlacek—so devoted to Christian values—shot and killed his Pastor.

Scott Roeder of Kansas heard from Bill O'Reilly's television show that local Doctor George Tiller performed legal abortions, including (still legal in Kansas) late-term abortion. Actually, O'Reilly called Tiller a 'mass murderer' and 'Tiller the baby killer.' Mr. Roeder, obviously upset at this violation of 'Thou Shalt Not Kill' took it upon himself to kill Dr. Tiller, in his own church, no less.

Richard Poplowski, a Christian, heard on (wait for it ...) Fox News that President Obama and the Democratic Party planned to take his guns. It wasn't true, but he killed 3 cops anyway.

When you believe you are absolutely on the side of the one true God, it's easy to believe that anyone who opposes you is on the side of Satan. And if you believe someone who disagrees with you is on the side of Satan, then anything you do to stop them is ordained by the Almighty.

American Christians have been fed a lie—that as long as you believe that Christ was literally crucified and rose from the dead, you can ignore everything He actually preached and call yourself His follower. This explains so much about so many people in this country. And that's why Keith Giles' book matters.

Keith calls out the hypocrites with facts, logic and scripture itself. *Jesus Unarmed* shows that the Christ of the Bible doesn't allow too much wiggle room when it comes to violence.

These days, Christian gun enthusiasts have new ammo in the fight to prove you can be a follower of Jesus while also enjoying weapons designed to kill lots of people. It's Luke 22:36, also known as "sell your cloak a buy a sword." And it's quickly become a mantra for fun-loving, gun-loving, Father-and-the-Son-loving Christians. And whether you believe in Jesus in any literal, metaphorical or spiritual way, you may encounter this talking point.

In *Jesus Unarmed*, Keith takes on this story and shows us that while Jesus never comes out against owning swords, he seriously comes out against using them on people. Jesus carries a high capacity for love and forgiveness, not a high-capacity magazine.

Of course, if Jesus had an AR-15 he could've mowed down the Romans, never be crucified, never had a religion named for him, and none of us would ever know who Pat Robertson was. But I'll leave the Bible Fan Fiction to the Left Behind books.

There's a word for people whose religious opinions make them believe they're above the law, and that violence and murder in the name of their faith are morally justified: Terrorist.

But, unlike Islamic terrorism, which targets Christians, Jews, and other Muslims, US Christian Terrorism targets our fellow Americans.

Whenever you mix social injustice, ignorance and religious charismatics telling people who to blame for their problems, you're going to get violence. Whether it's a mullah telling impoverished people in the oil-rich Middle East to blame their suffering on Jews and the Great Satan of America, or a Christian preacher telling struggling Americans that gays, abortionists and liberals are moral evils—and that their version of God's law trumps man's—terrorism will be the symptom.

No real Christian would defend brutality and violence—just as no sincere Muslim defends terrorism either. These people are not followers of Christ, they are the Christian American Taliban. And Jesus is not their teacher, he's their prop.

I've always believed the best weapon for refuting Bible Thumpers is usually the Bible. Because the only way you can cling to both a Bible and a gun is if you totally agree to not read the Jesus parts.

Take this book and use it well.

– John Fugelsang
Host of "Tell Me Everything", Sirius XM Radio

INTRODUCTION

"It is only when a mosquito lands on his testicles that a man realizes there is always a way to solve problems without using violence."

— CONFUSCIUS

"I'd say a quarter to a half of our [Church] members are concealed carry. They have guns and I don't think there's anything wrong with that. They bring them into the church with them, and if somebody tries that [a shooting] in our church, they may get one shot off, or two shots off, but that's it—and that's the last thing they'll ever do in this life."

— PASTOR ROBERT JEFFRESS, FIRST BAPTIST CHURCH, DALLAS, TX[1]

As far back as I can remember, all of my heroes carried guns; Marshall Dillon on Gunsmoke, James West on the Wild Wild West, John Wayne, even Captain Kirk, they were all always ready to respond with violence whenever necessary—and it seemed as if it was always necessary each and every week I tuned in to my favorite television shows.

Early on I got the message: Good guys use violence to stop the bad guys and protect the innocent. Or, as it has been communicated in recent times, "The only thing that can stop a bad man with a gun is a good man with a gun."

This myth of redemptive violence runs deep in our American psyche. We used violence to earn our independence from Britain. We used violence to end the practice of slavery. In fact, without at least some form of violence, almost nothing in U.S. history has ever been accomplished.

> EARLY ON I GOT THE MESSAGE: GOOD GUYS USE VIOLENCE TO STOP THE BAD GUYS AND PROTECT THE INNOCENT. OR, AS IT HAS BEEN COMMUNICATED IN RECENT TIMES, "THE ONLY THING THAT CAN STOP A BAD MAN WITH A GUN IS A GOOD MAN WITH A GUN."

Since 1776, America has been at war for 222 years out of 239 years, or approximately 93 percent of our history.[2] Simply put, we are violent nation.

So, it's hardly any wonder that our heroes are violent men who carry weapons and overcome evil using deadly force whenever necessary. It's in our DNA as a nation. We are addicted to violence. We are convinced that violence can be redemptive and restorative. In fact, we are so convinced of this that we find it very difficult to believe that God is nonviolent, or that Jesus would want us to behave nonviolently.

I can remember the first time this notion of nonviolence ever entered my mind. As a young boy who loved watching television in the Seventies—shows like Starsky and Hutch, Mannix, and S.W.A.T.—I came across a rather odd detective show starring George Peppard called "Banachek." What set this show apart from every single other cop show on television was the fact that the main character never carried a gun. Ever.

That really shocked me. Suddenly I began to consider the possibility that it was actually possible to overcome evil without a weapon of any kind. Not only that, it might even take a stronger man—a more brave and courageous one—without holding a gun, or a knife, or anything at all other than a sense of justice and a desire to expose the darkness using only the light of truth.

Still, as paradigm-shifting as it was for my young mind to ponder these things, I never stopped believing in the power of redemptive violence. In fact, I was always running around playing cowboys and Indians or cops and robbers. Most of my favorite toys were handguns or rifles. I can remember having a .357 magnum gun (just like Hutch used on Starsky and Hutch), and a snub nose .38 with a real metal cylinder that rotated and fired caps (just like the one used by Baretta), and a flintlock pistol and rifle set (just like Davy Crocket used), and a machine gun (just like Eliot Ness used), and even an official Star Trek phaser pistol (just like Kirk used).

Truth be told, I was almost never found without a toy gun—or three—somewhere on my person. I kept a pistol in my sock under my boots, and another pistol in the back of my waistband, and yet a third one under my armpit in a makeshift holster I had rigged inside my jacket. At five years old, I was deadly.

More than once I got caught carrying a toy gun like this. The worst time was when we were about to board an airplane and I had to admit to my dad I had a realistic looking handgun in my boot. When he showed it to the TSA officer they nearly tackled my dad to the ground because it looked so real. Then they confiscated it and I watched them melt it inside a microwave behind the desk to destroy it.

Of course, when we got to where we were going we swung by the toy store to replace my revolver with one that looked just like it.

Looking back on my own childhood I can see why so many of us today are enamored with the idea that guns are what good guys need to stop the bad guys. Between every toy commercial, tv show, movie, comic, and book I've ever read, the message is reinforced over and over again: *Violence is necessary to protect us from evil.* Case closed. No question. End of story.

But, is it the end of the story? Is it really true that the more guns we have the safer we are from evil, violence and crime? Is violence the most effective tool we have? Is it really true that we could make the world a better place by just killing enough bad people?

There was a time in my life when I would have answered "Yes" to every one of those questions above. Now, I'm not so sure. Why? Well, mostly because of Jesus and his example, and his teaching. But also because of the overwhelming evidence we have that demonstrates to us that redemptive violence is not only *not* the answer, it's actually part of the problem. In fact, it might actually be *the* problem we need to solve before we can advance as a species and move beyond the Stone Age.

MIMETIC RIVALRY

Human beings are mimetic creatures. That is to say, we reflexively behave the way others behave around us and are influenced by others to desire what they desire. In other words, our actions and our desires are not truly our own. We inherently learn what we should value based on what we see others seeking after.

This is why marketing works. If it didn't work, then the advertising industry worldwide wouldn't be raking in billions of dollars every month basing their business model on this very same principle. So, if people see that Lady Gaga wears this dress, or if Taylor Swift drinks this brand of soda, or if any other celebrity identifies with a certain fashion, or automobile, or what have you, we tend to purchase those same things. Why? Partly because we want to be as cool as they are, but primarily because of this instinctive mechanism buried deep within every single one of us—mimetic desire.

On a very personal level I can remember the first time I consciously experienced this. My friend Lee Hammar was the coolest guy I knew when I was in college. He had short spiky hair and played bass guitar in a band and he wrote his own songs and sang lead vocals. He also wore black shoes and black jeans. All the time. I can remember making a point to go out shopping for a pair of black shoes and black jeans because I wanted to look like Lee Hammar. Later on, I joined a band and sang lead vocals. I cut my hair short and I spiked it. Why? Well, now it's plainly obvious: I wanted to be as much like the coolest guy I knew. Truth be told it was only until around 5 years ago that I stopped wearing black shoes. I still only wear black jeans to this very day.

Our mimetic tendencies actually serve a very practical purpose. Without this mechanism, no infant could ever learn to talk, or walk. This built-in mimesis allows children to quickly speak whatever language they are born into and to laugh at what their parents laugh at, eat what their parents eat, dress like their parents, behave like their parents and adopt the customs of their parents. Those same children also learn to mimic the attitudes, likes, dislikes, and a variety of other traits from their peers.

Mimetic desire works in much the same way. Place one toddler alone in a room full of toys. Watch them naturally gravitate towards one or two playthings on the floor. Now, introduce another toddler. Watch that child pick up a different toy and begin to play with it. Now observe that first child's reaction. As the child sees that the toy it had previously ignored is now bringing so much joy to the other child, a single word begins to rise up in his throat: "Mine!"

This is mimetic desire and we all have it, even if we don't realize it. It secretly drives our behaviors in ways we can't even detect. But, once we can see how this mimetic desire affects our actions, we at least have an opportunity to address it.

It was French author and literature professor, Rene Girard, who famously unveiled this truth to the academic and theological world several years ago. In his book, *I See Satan Fall Like Lightning*, he expounds on the problem of mimetic desire and how it leads to mimetic rivalry, which ultimately leads to conflict and violence.

Simply put, Girard not only demonstrated that humanity is always at the mercy of their own mimetic desires, but that this is exactly what is being communicated in the Ten Commandments.

As Girard notes, six of the ten "Thou Shalt Not" commands in the Law of Moses have to do with mimetic desires: Do not desire any other gods but Yahweh. Do not commit adultery (which is about desiring someone other than your own spouse). Do not covet (desire) your neighbor's wife. Do not covet (desire) anything that belongs to your neighbor. Do not steal (which is the fruit of wanting something that is not yours). Do not kill (which is often the result of a conflict over something you and another person both desire).[3]

So, right from the beginning, the scriptures reveal to us that we, as humans, struggle most with this tendency to desire things that others desire. In effect, we are being told that one of our most fundamental struggles as people stems from our mimesis, and if we study the fruits of mimetic desire we'll see that it often leads to conflict, and these conflicts often lead to violence and bloodshed and even war.

This means our tendency towards violence is linked to a very human mechanism that most of us are not aware of and nearly all of us are helpless to resist. Violence, it seems, is coded into our DNA.

But, is this the end of the story? Is there no hope for us to escape our predisposition towards violence? Well, even though I am mostly a pessimist at heart, I have to say that, in this case, I have very high hopes for a way out of our mimetic rivalry and conflicts that lead us to violence. In fact, I believe it's one of the primary things that Jesus came to rescue us from.

That's what this book is all about. I hope you'll find some peace in these next few pages, and develop your own hope for another way to be human that doesn't involve an eye for an eye, or a tooth for a tooth. Jesus has a better idea, and he's already revealed the secret to us. We just need to know what we're looking for. So, I hope you're ready for what's next. It may involve rethinking some of your assumptions. It might mean rethinking ideas and reconsidering scriptures and revaluating theology in ways you've never considered before. But, in the end, I believe you'll find it all worthwhile.

Let's get started.

"IF WE COULD READ THE SECRET HISTORY OF OUR ENEMIES, WE SHOULD FIND IN EACH MAN'S LIFE SORROW AND SUFFERING ENOUGH TO DISARM ALL HOSTILITY."

- HENRY WADSWORTH LONGFELLOW

CHAPTER 1

WILL THE PRINCE OF PEACE PLEASE STAND UP?

"We are up to the hilt advocates for peace, and we earnestly war against war. I wish that Christian men would insist more and more on the unrighteousness of war, believing that Christianity means no sword, no cannon, no bloodshed, and that, if a nation is driven to fight in its own defense, Christianity stands by to weep and to intervene as soon as possible, and not to join in the cruel shouts which celebrate an enemy's slaughter."

— CHARLES SPURGEON[4]

"If we want a world in which we finally lay down our instruments of war—whether they be words or weapons—it only begins when the peace we celebrate becomes the peace that incarnates."

— BRANDON ANDRESS

Before we get too deep into this topic, I think it's very important to establish a few things up front: namely, the notion that Jesus is a nonviolent Messiah who actually taught that we should take his example of enemy-love seriously if we intend to become one of his disciples.

The reason I feel the need to stress this is because, quite often, I find myself in debates with other Christians—and it's always other Christians who seek to argue with me on this topic—about the idea that Jesus really was, and is, nonviolent.

Of course, it depends on whether or not the debate is against other religions, like Islam, for example, or if the debate is simply about whether or not Jesus was serious about loving our enemies rather than killing them.

Apparently, if the conversation is about contrasting Christianity with Islam, these Christians are quick to quote all of those nonviolent passages as proof that their faith is peaceful as they cherry-pick the most violent verses they can Google from the Qur'an. But, if the conversation is specifically about whether or not Jesus was anti-violence and committed to peacemaking, then suddenly these same Christians want to "balance" things by pointing out that Jesus made a whip to chase out the moneychangers from the Temple, and that he flipped over tables, and that he's coming back one day soon with a sword coming out of his mouth to slaughter his enemies. So, which is it? Is Christianity a religion of peace, or is it one where the Messiah is committed to making his enemies bleed?

SO, WHICH IS IT? IS CHRISTIANITY A RELIGION OF PEACE, OR IS IT ONE WHERE THE MESSIAH IS COMMITTED TO MAKING HIS ENEMIES BLEED?

To me, the overwhelming evidence from both the Old and the New Testament scriptures is plainly obvious. Jesus was and is and will always be the Prince of Peace. He says, "Blessed are the peacemakers, for they will be called the children of God." (Matt. 5:9) He reveals to us a God who is not wrathful or angry but who is, instead, full of mercy, forgiveness and grace for all of us—even those who consider themselves the enemies of God. (Luke 6:27-36; 15:11-32)

Still, it has always puzzled me why so many Christians seem to dispute the claim that Jesus was a nonviolent messiah, or that he called us as his disciples to behave nonviolently, too. I've often said that the only people who seem to have trouble admitting that Jesus taught nonviolence are Christians. Nonbelievers, those of other faiths, even Atheists and Agnostics, freely embrace Jesus of Nazareth as the originator of the modern notion of nonviolent resistance. For example, when someone like Bill Maher—a self-avowed Atheist who has gone out of his way to attack and even try to debunk Christianity—makes an observation like this (below), we have to admit that we may have a blind spot when it comes to Jesus and nonviolence:

> "New rule: If you're a Christian who supports killing your enemies and torture, you have to come up with a new name for yourself … Non-violence was kind of Jesus' trademark. Kind of his big thing. To not follow that part of it is like joining Greenpeace and hating whales. I mean, you know, there's interpreting and then there's just ignoring. It's ignoring if you're for torture, as are more Evangelical Christians than any other religion … Martin Luther King, Jr. gets to call himself a Christian because he actually practiced loving his enemies."[5]

So, the question, "Why do Christians seem to be the only ones who doubt that Jesus was nonviolent?" seems to point to a large disconnect in how we see Jesus, and in what we understand the Gospel to be about. For many Christians, it's not Jesus or the Sermon on the Mount they actively follow. It's the Apostle Paul and the Evangelical

FOR MANY CHRISTIANS, IT'S NOT JESUS OR THE SERMON ON THE MOUNT THEY ACTIVELY FOLLOW. IT'S THE APOSTLE PAUL AND THE EVANGELICAL VERSION OF CHRISTIANITY THAT HAS MORE TO DO WITH PRAYING A PRAYER SO YOU CAN GO TO HEAVEN WHEN YOU DIE.

version of Christianity that has more to do with praying a prayer so you can go to Heaven when you die. We tend to communicate the Gospel, not how Jesus explains it in those four books called "The Gospels", but as Paul appears to do in 1 Corinthians 15:1-7. This leads us to miss what Jesus was saying entirely and to substitute a version of the Gospel that is primarily focused on getting people to Heaven and less about what Jesus cared about: helping us to love God and love others as he loved us.[6]

In America, especially, the Evangelical Christian faith has morphed into a twisted mutation that allows people to hold tight to their Second Amendment rights and to ignore the enemy-love commands of Jesus without ever asking what Jesus meant when he asked, "why do you call me 'Lord, lord' and do not do what I say?" Obedience to the red letters of the four Gospels has become not merely a secondary consideration, it is not even a consideration at all. This leads us to pledge allegiance to the State and to identify ourselves more as Americans who vote a certain way rather than as devoted followers of Christ who base everything they do on one of the direct teachings of Jesus from the Sermon on the Mount.[7]

Of course, as some of these same Christians love to point out, there are legitimate objections to the assertion that Jesus was truly teaching us to behave nonviolently and these are based on what appears to be scriptural evidence to the contrary. This book will absolutely look at each and every one of those verses in detail, rest assured. But, for now, let's simply take a moment to admit that the plain doctrine of Jesus was this: Love your enemies, bless those who curse you, do good to those who hate you and overcome evil with good. And why? Because, Jesus tells us, to do so is to be like your Heavenly Father.

In other words, because God loves His enemies this way, you should love your enemies this way, too. It's pretty straightforward.

Or, to put it another way: God loves all the people you hate and wants you to love them, too.

To be honest, it's this very teaching that sets Jesus apart from everyone else. His radical assertion that we should not merely tolerate our enemies but preemptively and proactively love them is breath-takingly audacious, astoundingly profound and bristling with transcendent insight that defies human understanding. Yet, it's also very practical once you really begin to consider it.

Humanity has, from the very beginning, responded to violence with more violence. When someone insults us, we insult them right back. When they strike us, we strike back. When they kill someone we love, we kill two of theirs. When they wipe out our family, we annihilate their entire village. When they attack our nation, we obliterate every man, woman and child on their side. Where does it all end? It ends, inevitably, in genocide on a worldwide scale. Surely, there must be a better way than this? Well, there is a better way—and don't call me Shirley.

Seriously, Jesus is the one who shows us both the futility of our way of responding to violence and suggests the only possible way of breaking the endless cycle of escalation that leads to our own destruction. He shows us a new and better way—the way of love—that leads to peace, and joy and to life.

Take a moment and read through this section of his Sermon on the Mount and you'll see what I'm talking about:

> "But I say to you who hear, Love your enemies, do good to those who hate you, bless those who curse you, pray for those who abuse you. To one who strikes you on the cheek, offer the other also, and from one who takes away your cloak do not withhold your tunic either. Give to everyone who begs from you, and from one who takes away your goods do not demand them back. And as you wish that others would do to you, do so to them.

"If you love those who love you, what benefit is that to you? For even sinners love those who love them. And if you do good to those who do good to you, what benefit is that to you? For even sinners do the same. And if you lend to those from whom you expect to receive, what credit is that to you? Even sinners lend to sinners, to get back the same amount. But love your enemies, and do good, and lend, expecting nothing in return, and your reward will be great, and you will be sons of the Most High, for he is kind to the ungrateful and the evil. Be merciful, even as your Father is merciful." (Luke 6:27-36)

As we read these words, we should find our perspectives on what it means to be a follower of Jesus shifting. If Jesus is serious about these instructions to his disciples—and I am fully convinced that he is—then we have to be willing to reconsider our ideas of what it means to be a Christian.

Make no mistake, Jesus really is the Prince of Peace. He really does intend for us to take these words to heart and—better yet—put them into actual practice in our daily lives. Without it, we will always remain enslaved to our own mimetic desires that lead us to conflict, violence, war and death.

However, I do feel the need to clarify that what Jesus is calling us into is not what most of us think of as Pacifism which is quite often thought of as "doing nothing" in the face of violence. Jesus is most certainly not advocating that any of us respond to evil, injustice or violence by sitting idly by and doing nothing. But, there is a large spectrum of action for Christians to employ between the extremes of responding violently or doing nothing at all. We have to explore what those other options may be and enter into a creative reimagination of what it looks like for us to follow Jesus into this new nonviolent resistance to evil as a means of disarming the oppressor and ultimately seeking the redemption and transformation of everyone involved.

Maybe we should take some time to dig a little deeper into the nonviolent teachings of Jesus to establish the scope of his commitment to practicing nonviolence and preemptive love before we try to answer those common objections raised by Bible-believing Christians who cite scripture to the contrary.

That's what we'll do in our next chapter.

CHAPTER 2

WAS JESUS REALLY SERIOUS?

"The whole point of the Kingdom of God is Jesus has come to bear witness to the true truth, which is nonviolent. When God wants to take charge of the world, He doesn't send in the tanks. He sends in the poor and the meek."

— N.T. WRIGHT

As we've already pointed out, there are those who challenge the notion that Jesus was actually nonviolent. In fact, I can vividly remember when a pastor once told me that if I was going to try to tell him that Jesus taught nonviolence, he was prepared to punch me in the face. No kidding. In fact, that interaction was part of what opened my eyes to the fact that there are hundreds, maybe even thousands, of pastors in pulpits across this nation who are loudly proclaiming the gospel of redemptive violence and shouting down anyone who might suggest that Jesus wasn't a violent messiah. That should really disturb us. It certainly disturbs me.

So, before we dive into our chapters debunking the myth of redemptive violence let's take some time to examine the question of whether or not Jesus really did teach nonviolence, and if he seriously expected us to live out this proactive love ethic as evidence of our faith in him.

When we take a look at who Jesus was, we should back up to those Old Testament prophecies concerning the Messiah who was to come and look closely at what it was this "Anointed One" was expected to accomplish. If we do that, we'll undoubtedly come across this passage in the book of Isaiah where we read:

> "In the last days the mountain of the LORD's temple will be established as the highest of the mountains; it will be exalted above the hills, and all nations will stream to it. Many peoples will come and say, "Come, let us go up to the mountain of the LORD, to the temple of the God of Jacob. *He will teach us his ways, so that we may walk in his paths.*" The law will go out from Zion, *the word of the LORD from Jerusalem.* He will judge between the nations and will settle disputes for many peoples. *They will beat their swords into plowshares and their spears into pruning hooks. Nation will not take up sword against nation, nor will they train for war anymore.*" (Isaiah 2:2-4, emphasis mine)

Notice here that the Messiah who comes will "teach us his ways, so that we may walk in his paths." So, did Jesus do this? Did Jesus "teach us his ways"? Yes, he did. Where? In the Sermon on the Mount found in chapters 5 through 7 in the Gospel of Matthew. This is where Jesus lays out his manifesto and explains how we should live life in the Kingdom of God. Notice also that the reason Jesus will "teach us his ways" is specifically "so that we may walk in his paths." It's not merely a teaching for us to memorize or study. It's a path for us to walk in our everyday lives. And, if we do start to walk in this path laid for us by Jesus in his Sermon on the Mount, what will be the fruit of this? "They will beat their swords into plowshares and their spears into pruning hooks." So, if and only if, we begin to walk in this path laid out for us by Jesus, we will become people who make up their minds to repurpose our weapons of violence; turning them from implements of death into tools for creating life, sustenance and nourishment that can be shared with everyone.

I cannot tell you how many times I have heard Christians respond to this verse by pointing out that "No one is doing this today, so this prophecy hasn't been fulfilled yet." They're waiting for Jesus to come back the second time to make this reality happen. But, the problem is,

JESUS ONLY PROVIDES THE TEACHING AND POINTS OUT THE PATH FOR US. WE ARE THE ONES WHO HAVE TO PUT THIS TEACHING INTO PRACTICE. WE ARE THE ONES WHO NEED TO WALK THIS PATH.

they're missing the entire point of the Isaiah prophecy. It's not Jesus who makes this happen. Jesus only provides the teaching and points out the path for us. We are the ones who have to put this teaching into practice. We are the ones who need to walk this path. We are the ones who must decide to trade our violent weapons in for tools of peace. Or, to put it another way, "The world will only change if we change."

This parable I wrote may help illustrate what I'm talking about a little better:

> There was a wise man who told the people: "When wisdom comes to you, you will share your bread and your water with everyone who is hungry and thirsty." The people looked around and saw that no one around them was sharing their food or water. So, they decided to wait and pray for that day when this wisdom would finally come and then everyone who is thirsty would drink and everyone who was hungry would eat. The people sang songs about that day when this wisdom might come. They searched the skies for signs of the coming wisdom. Eventually, those who were thirsty died and those who were hungry wasted away. And the people continued to wait, and sing, and pray.

Hopefully, you can see how misguided it is to hear such a simple teaching and mistake it for an opportunity to sit back and wait for God to "make it all happen," when the entire point is for us to be the ones who incarnate this teaching in order to become the fulfillment we are waiting to manifest.

Here's another Messianic prophecy pointing to the coming Christ that we should examine:

> "In the past he humbled the land of Zebulun and the land of Naphtali, but *in the future [God] will honor Galilee of the nations, by the Way of the Sea, beyond the Jordan—The people walking in darkness have seen a great light; on those living in the land of deep darkness a light has dawned* ...

> "... *Every warrior's boot used in battle and every garment rolled in blood will be destined for burning, will be fuel for the fire.*

> "*For to us a child is born, to us a son is given, and the government will be on his shoulders. And he will be called:* Wonderful Counselor, Mighty God, Everlasting Father, *Prince of Peace.* (Isaiah 9:1-6, emphasis mine)

Once more, we see examples of how this coming Messiah would cause "every warrior's boot used in battle and every garment rolled in blood" to become "fuel for the fire," because, as in the previous passage, the people have "seen a great light" and now that this "light has dawned" on them, they awaken to the foolishness of war and recognize it as a reminder of the time when they were once "living in the land of deep darkness."

This is why they can legitimately proclaim that this child who would be born would be hailed by everyone as—among other things—the "Prince of Peace."

There is one other significant Messianic prophecy found in the book of Isaiah that we will get to shortly. But, for now, let's turn our attention to the scriptures that speak about the nonviolent Jesus more directly: The Gospels.

GOOD NEWS FOR EVERYONE

When the Gospel of Luke introduces us to Jesus, it's with the sound of a multitude of angelic host who proclaim his birth to the lowly shepherds in the field, saying:

> "Do not be afraid. I bring you good news that will cause *great joy for all the people*. Today in the town of David a Savior has been born to you; he is the Messiah, the Lord. This will be a sign to you: You will find a baby wrapped in cloths and lying in a manger."

> Suddenly a great company of the heavenly host appeared with the angel, praising God and saying: "Glory to God in the highest heaven, *and on earth peace to those on whom his favor rests.*" (Luke 2:10-14, emphasis mine)

As we've already seen, the Messiah to come was prophesied in Isaiah to be the "Prince of Peace" whose teachings would lead us to follow the path that results in the decision to "study war no more" and to "beat our swords into plowshares." This announcement of the birth of Jesus to the shepherds in the field confirms the identity, calling and mission of the Anointed One: to bring peace on the earth.

TRUE CHILDREN OF GOD

When Jesus begins his ministry, his first and most compelling sermon is recorded in the Gospel of Luke where he calls his disciples to walk in this same path of peace:

> "Blessed are the merciful, for they will be shown mercy. Blessed are the pure in heart, for they shall see God. *Blessed are the peacemakers, for they shall be called the sons of God.*" (Luke 5:7-9)

This idea of being called the sons of God, or the children of God, is directly related to how one's actions and thoughts mirror the Father's. In other words, when we follow the example of God, we show that we are truly the children of God. "Like Father, like son," as the saying goes. Jesus confirms this way of thinking when he rebukes the Pharisees who claim Abraham as their father (ancestor) by pointing out that, if they were truly the sons of Abraham they would be doing the things that he did:

> "If you were Abraham's children," said Jesus, "then you would do what Abraham did. As it is, you are looking for a way to kill me, a man who has told you the truth that I heard from God. Abraham did not do such things. You are doing the works of your own father."

> "We are not illegitimate children," they protested. "The only Father we have is God himself."

> Jesus said to them, "If God were your Father, you would love me, for I have come here from God. I have not come on my own; God sent me. Why is my language not clear to you? Because you are unable to hear what I say. You belong to your father, the devil, and you want to carry out your father's desires. He was a murderer from the beginning, not holding to the truth, for there is no truth in him. When he lies, he speaks his native language, for he is a liar and the father of lies." (John 8:39-44)

So, when Jesus says, in is Sermon on the Mount, that those who become peacemakers are the sons of God, this is exactly what he's talking about. To make peace is to be like your Father, who is also working to bring peace. Jesus also carries forward this same idea later in his teaching when he suggests that we should love our enemies simply because this is what God does:

> "You have heard that it was said, 'Eye for eye, and tooth for tooth.' But I tell you, do not resist an evil person. If anyone slaps you on the right cheek, turn to them the other cheek also. And if anyone wants to sue you and take your shirt, hand over your coat as well. If anyone forces you to go one mile, go with them

two miles. Give to the one who asks you, and do not turn away
from the one who wants to borrow from you.

"You have heard that it was said, 'Love your neighbor and hate
your enemy.' *But I tell you, love your enemies and pray for those
who persecute you, that you may be children of your Father in
heaven. He causes his sun to rise on the evil and the good, and
sends rain on the righteous and the unrighteous.* If you love those
who love you, what reward will you get? Are not even the tax
collectors doing that? And if you greet only your own people,
what are you doing more than others? Do not even pagans
do that? *Be Holy, therefore, as your heavenly Father is Holy."*
(Matthew 5:38-48)

One key idea that needs to be understood in this passage
is how Jesus is redefining our idea of "Holiness." Because the
Pharisees believed that God's Holiness separated God from the
"sinners" of the world; personified in those who were poor and
sick, or those who engaged in sinful activities such as drunken-
ness, prostitution or tax collecting, for example, they also did
their best to avoid contact with
these same filthy sinners. However,
Jesus turns this concept of God's
Holiness upside down and shows us,
instead, a God whose love for the
unrighteous is equal to his love for
the righteous ones. Then, and only
then, does Jesus urge us to "be Holy,
therefore, as your heavenly Father is
Holy." In other words, God is not
too Holy to love the unrighteous,

> JESUS TURNS THIS CONCEPT
> OF GOD'S HOLINESS UPSIDE
> DOWN AND SHOWS US,
> INSTEAD, A GOD WHOSE
> LOVE FOR THE UNRIGHTEOUS
> IS EQUAL TO HIS LOVE FOR
> THE RIGHTEOUS ONES. THEN,
> AND ONLY THEN, DOES
> JESUS URGE US TO "BE
> HOLY, THEREFORE, AS YOUR
> HEAVENLY FATHER IS HOLY."

and this means you're not either. If God expresses his Holiness
by how much love, mercy and grace is poured out on them,
then if we hope to be like our Heavenly Father, we should do
the same. This is what it means to be Holy as God is Holy. It has

nothing to do with being perfectly sinless and everything to do with expressing unconditional love to everyone around us.

OUR FIRM FOUNDATION

At the conclusion of Jesus's manifesto on what it looks like to follow him and live as a citizen of the Kingdom of God, he shares an interesting parable of sorts to illustrate an important point:

> "Therefore *everyone who hears these words of mine and puts them into practice* is like a wise man who built his house on the rock. The rain came down, the streams rose, and the winds blew and beat against that house; yet it did not fall, because it had its foundation on the rock. But *everyone who hears these words of mine and does not put them into practice* is like a foolish man who built his house on sand. The rain came down, the streams rose, and the winds blew and beat against that house, and it fell with a great crash." (Matt. 7:24-26, emphasis mine)

Notice that the emphasis here is not on whether or not someone hears the words of Jesus, but in whether or not they put those words into practice. Many times we tend act as if knowing what Jesus said is enough. But what Jesus says here, and elsewhere, is that putting his words into practice—orthopraxy—is much more essential than knowing what he said—orthodoxy. This same idea is also stressed in the Gospel of John where Jesus washes the feet of his disciples, urges them to wash one another's feet, and then says this: *"Now that you know these things, you will be blessed if you do them."* (John 13:17) So, it's not when we know something that we are blessed. Rather, it is only when we put what we know into practice that we reap the benefits of that "knowing." Which is why Jesus also asks us, "Why do you call me 'Lord, lord' and do not do the things I say?" (Luke 6:46)

Please understand, the point of this is not to place a burden on us or to make us feel guilty for not doing enough to earn

God's favor or love. Not at all. The point is simply to show us how important it is for us to not merely believe Jesus, but that this belief bear the fruit of transformation within that results in a change of heart and mind, and therefore, our actions, too.

As I like to say, "Swimming won't make you a fish, but if you're a fish you will swim." That's the entire point. It's not about doing good things to become righteous. It's simply about experiencing the inner transformation and renovation of the heart that comes from knowing Christ and abiding in him daily. As we begin to rest in Christ who resides in us, our hearts begin to change. Our thoughts become as his. Our actions mirror God's actions. We inevitably become like our Father in heaven and because we are God's children, we cannot help but love as God loves, serve as God serves, and forgive as God forgives. It doesn't happen all at once, but it does absolutely happen.

This, again, is why the prophecy in Isaiah foretells a transformation in those who walk in the path of the Messiah so that they eventually decide to lay down their weapons and study war no longer. Following the Prince of Peace makes them peaceful. Listening to the God who is Love makes them loving. They cannot help themselves. They are becoming like their Father in heaven who brings sweet, refreshing rain on those who hate and curse his name. The transformation of the heart is underway.

DONKEYS AND PALM BRANCHES

When Jesus rides into Jerusalem on what we now refer to as "Palm Sunday" we see another example of this Prince of Peace in action.

On the day that the Passover Lamb was traditionally selected, Jesus rode into Jerusalem on a donkey. Spontaneously, the people along the road began to wave palm branches and shout

"Hosanna!" but what's really going on might surprise you. First of all, the people received Jesus as a prophet (Matt. 21:11) but not as the Messiah.

This event was prophesied in Zechariah 9:9:

> "Rejoice greatly, Daughter Zion! Shout, Daughter Jerusalem! See, your king comes to you, righteous and victorious, lowly and riding on a donkey, on a colt, the foal of a donkey."

The truth is that the rest of that prophecy was about the Messiah coming as an agent of peace:

> "I will take away the chariots from Ephraim and the warhorses from Jerusalem, and the battle bow will be broken. He will proclaim peace to the nations. His rule will extend from sea to sea and from the River to the ends of the earth." (v. 10)

Notice that Jesus weeps over the fact that they do not understand what his mission is when he responds to their adulation and palm-waving with this statement:

> "As he approached Jerusalem and saw the city, he wept over it and said, *"If you, even you, had only known on this day what would bring you peace*—but now it is hidden from your eyes. The days will come upon you when your enemies will build an embankment against you and encircle you and hem you in on every side. They will dash you to the ground, you and the children within your walls. They will not leave one stone on another, because you did not recognize the time of God's coming to you." (Luke 19:41-44, emphasis mine)

See, the fact that the people were waving palm branches is significant. Those palm branches were a direct throwback to the Maccabean period when the triumphant Jewish warriors rode into Jerusalem and the people celebrated their victory over the Seleucids, which incidentally was followed immediately by a ritual cleansing of the temple. At that time the people waved palm branches as a symbol of military conquest over an oppressive enemy. By waving those palm branches, the people are saying that they are ready for war. They are ready for the blood of the Romans to be spilled in an uprising that they hope Jesus will lead them in. It's no different than when Peter cut off the servant's ear in Gethsemane and received the rebuke from Jesus.

Today we usually read that passage about the people shouting "Hosanna!" as an indication that the people received Jesus as their King. But on the contrary, the people were rejecting Jesus as their personal, spiritual Messiah and calling out for him to be their political, militant Messiah. When they shout "Hosanna!" which means "Save us!" they are demanding him to lead the charge of attack against the Romans.

This is why Jesus weeps over the people. He knows that their hearts are far from God's heart. They want war. He has come to bring peace. They reject him and his mission. They can't receive him for who he is. They cannot submit to him as he is—a humble servant riding on a donkey—they only want him to meet their expectations for a warrior who will set them free from earthly oppression. But they are unwilling to be set free from their own lusts and desires.

Remember, this was traditionally the day that the Passover lamb was chosen to take away the sins of the people. Yet, on this day, the people rejected the Lamb because they wanted a Lion instead.

Ironically, the people of Jerusalem would receive the very punishment they sought to bring upon the Romans, as Jesus predicts in Luke 19:41-44, above.

Later in Luke 21:5-38, Jesus repeats this same warning in his Olivet Discourse, which is a warning about the coming destruction of the Temple in Jerusalem which, sadly, did occur in 70 A.D.

This is why Jesus weeps. He knows that, in about 40 years of time, the Romans will surround the city and kill everyone and destroy the very temple he is about to go and cleanse.

The cleansing of the temple that Jesus performs immediately after his entry into Jerusalem on the donkey echoes the Maccabean cleansing roughly 200 years before. But when Jesus cleanses the temple this time it is more than ceremonial. Instead, he chases out the corrupt money changers and the sellers of doves who were exploiting the poor, and he clears the floor that was intended to be a place of prayer for the nations.

So, when you wave a palm branch on Palm Sunday, you should know that it's a symbol of military power and conquest, not a symbol of humble devotion to the King who rides on a donkey to reign as the Prince of Peace in every human heart.

FIRE FROM HEAVEN

There's another revealing scene from the life of Jesus that illustrates how even his own disciples needed to rethink their ideas of what the Messiah was sent to accomplish:

> "And he sent messengers on ahead, who went into a Samaritan village to get things ready for him; but the people there did not welcome him, because he was heading for Jerusalem. *When the disciples James and John saw this, they asked, "Lord, do you want us to call fire down from heaven to destroy them?" But Jesus turned and rebuked them.*" (Luke 9:52-55, emphasis mine)

Here, we see Jesus correcting the notion that we are allowed to destroy our enemies. In some manuscripts, Jesus even adds to this rebuke the statement: *"You do not know what kind of spirit you are of, for the Son of Man did not come to destroy people's lives, but to save them."*

This further clarifies and contrasts, not only the mission of Jesus to bring life and peace to everyone—even the unrighteous ones—but also the difference in the sort of "spirit" we are of whenever we seek to destroy people we don't like. When we seek to bless those who curse us, we are of the spirit of Christ. When we desire to call down fire from heaven to destroy our enemies, we are of the spirit of Anti-Christ. This is an issue of the heart, and Jesus is clear in his rebuke that those who follow him do not seek to destroy anyone, for any reason. The spirit within us is the spirit that seeks to bring life, and peace, and joy to everyone we see. Why? Because this is what God is like and our desire is to be like our Father in heaven.

This image of "fire from heaven" is ironically the sign of God's Holy Spirit being poured out on all flesh at Pentecost in the book of Acts. In that case, however, this fire from heaven does not destroy anyone but, instead, fills everyone with such Holy Love that people begin to sell their property to feed people who, only hours before, were total strangers to them. This is the kind of fire God desires to call down from heaven on all of us; a fire that cleanses our hatred and transforms us into loving children of God. We'll return to this "fire from heaven" image a bit later in the book, so don't forget this one.

> WHEN WE SEEK TO BLESS THOSE WHO CURSE US, WE ARE OF THE SPIRIT OF CHRIST. WHEN WE DESIRE TO CALL DOWN FIRE FROM HEAVEN TO DESTROY OUR ENEMIES, WE ARE OF THE SPIRIT OF ANTI-CHRIST.

DISARMING HIS DISCIPLES

One of the more memorable passages in the Gospels is the one where Peter, full of zeal to protect Jesus and eager to get this revolution against the Roman occupation underway, swings his sword and cuts off the ear of one of those who come to arrest Jesus in the garden. This is when Jesus turns to Peter and says:

> "Put away your sword! For all who take the sword will perish by the sword." (Matt. 26:52)

What could be more clear than this? Jesus disarms Peter who was seeking to defend his innocent friend from violence, showing us that violence is not the way Jesus—or his followers—respond to violence. Or, as Martin Luther King, Jr. once said,

> "Returning hate for hate multiplies hate, adding deeper darkness to a night already devoid of stars. Darkness cannot drive out darkness; only light can do that. Hate cannot drive out hate, only love can do that."[8]

Later, when Jesus stands before Pilate, he adds another startling detail about why his disciples do not respond to violence with more violence:

> "My kingdom is not of this world. *If my kingdom were of this world, my servants would have been fighting,* that I might not be delivered over to the Jews. *But my kingdom is not from the world.*" (John 18:36, emphasis mine)

So, one of the primary evidences that we are not of this world, and that Christ's Kingdom is not of this world is simply this: *We do not fight.* This underscores the notion that, while there may be plenty of things in this world worth dying for, there is nothing in this world worth killing for.

We are of a different Kingdom, and a different Spirit. We do not call down fire from heaven to destroy those who oppose us. We do not take up weapons to protect ourselves from those who seek to take our lives. We are here to demonstrate a better way to live; a better way to love; a better way to be human. And this way that Jesus shows us is one that finds its blueprint in the very heart of a Father who is love.

Because we affirm that God is love, and because we have embraced the idea that we were all made in the image of love—including our oppressors—we cannot respond to violence with violence. We are compelled by the Spirit of Christ and his breath-taking example of unconditional, self-sacrificing love, to respond with love.

This extravagant love of Christ is on full and glorious display when he prays for those who are in the act of nailing him—an innocent man—to a Roman cross: *"Father forgive them for they know not what they do" (Luke 23:34)* And it is, again, revealed when this same Jesus rises from the dead and breathes over his disciples—who all deserted him in his hour of anguish—"Peace!" (John 20:21)

So, to summarize what we've learned so far: The Messiah who was prophesied (in Isaiah 9:6) to come and establish peace, and was called the Prince of Peace, and whose teachings would call men to beat their swords into plowshares and study war no more (Isaiah 2:4), whose birth was announced by a legion of angels proclaiming "Peace on Earth, Good will to all mankind!" (Luke 2:14), and who came as a baby, and who rode into Jerusalem on a donkey and wept over the city because they did "not know the things that make for peace" (Luke 19:39-42), and who taught that we should turn the other cheek, bless those who hate us, and love our enemies (Matt. 5:43-48), and who rebuked the disciples when they wanted to call down fire on those who opposed them saying, "you know not what spirit you are of" (Luke 9:55), and who disarmed Peter (Matt. 26:52), and who told Pilate that his "kingdom was not of this world, if it were (his) disciples would fight" (John 18:36), and who said "Father forgive them for they know not what they do" (Luke 23:34), and who rose from the dead saying "Peace!" to his disciples (John 20:21), is most certainly *not* okay with practicing any form of violence against another person.

But, what about all those other verses in the Bible where it really does appear that Jesus was violent, or that he was okay with his disciples carrying swords? And what about in Revelation where Jesus returns on a white stallion covered in blood, ready to slaughter his enemies once and for all?

That's what we'll cover in our next chapter.

CHAPTER 3

BUT WHAT ABOUT ... ?

"When the power of love overcomes the love of power, then the world will know peace."

– JIMI HENDRIX

Can I be honest with you? Every time a Christian responds to the numerous nonviolent teachings of Jesus by asking, "But what about ... ?", I cannot help but hear those objections as another way of asking: "What are the scenarios where I don't have to obey Jesus?" In other words, if our posture as Christ-followers was genuinely focused on how to best follow his teachings, then we wouldn't spend our time trying to discover situations where we wouldn't have to follow him.

It's like if Jesus says, "You shall not commit adultery" and our response to that is, "Well, what if my wife is in a coma and we haven't had sex for 5 years and her home care nurse is really beautiful and single and lonely? Can I disobey Jesus now?" To me, this is exactly the same thing as hearing Jesus say "Love your enemies, bless those who curse you, if they strike your face, turn the other cheek ... " and our response is, "Okay, but what if there's a guy in my house with a gun to my wife's head? Can I blow his brains out now?"

These imaginary scenarios are invented to either cast doubt on the practicality of Jesus's teachings, or to find a loophole in the teaching where we don't really have to follow what Jesus says. This is curious behavior for those who contend to be Christ-like disciples who are committed to following Jesus.

To this I can only hear Jesus asking us, "Why do you call me 'Lord, lord' and yet do not do the things I say?" Still, I get it. We are confused by this teaching. It goes against the grain of everything we've ever been told about good versus evil, right and wrong, and godly justice. So, we bristle at the idea of turning our other cheek to brace for the second slap. We shudder at the thought of enduring an insult with a smile rather than firing back a zinger of our own. It just doesn't "feel" right to us. So, we struggle to follow Jesus into this nonviolent, enemy-loving territory because it simply does not compute. Therefore, Jesus must have been speaking metaphorically. Or maybe he was trying to show us how impossible it is to keep his commands and that must mean we shouldn't even try. Or perhaps Jesus is the only person who could ever love and forgive this way—because, after all, he's God in the flesh and I'm not—so it's not really practical for me to try to love in such a radical fashion.

But, I am convinced that Jesus really did mean for us to follow his example of love for our enemies. In fact, doing so is the only way we can demonstrate that we have been transformed from the inside out into people who are—like him—empowered to love those who hate us and bless those who curse us. Jesus said that to do so was to be like our Heavenly Father. So, refusal to do so is a denial of our true identity as children of God.

For many Christians, the scriptures themselves are what add to their confusion about Jesus's nonviolent instructions. Since they're already questioning whether or not Jesus could actually be serious about these ideas, when they run across a few verses in the New Testament that seem to confirm their suspicions that Jesus wasn't totally all-in on this "love your enemy" thing, they underline those passages and ignore the rest.

So, let's look a bit closer at those scriptures that most-often get quoted whenever someone suggests that Jesus was a nonviolent Messiah who called us to love our enemies.

TURNING OVER TABLES?

For me personally, this is probably the most common objection I hear. Mostly because Jesus acts in a way that appears to be violent. Therefore, they conclude, violence is an acceptable option for Christians. But is that really what's going on? A closer look reveals otherwise.

In context, the act of overturning the tables in the Temple comes immediately after another Messianic event—the triumphal entrance into Jerusalem on the back of a donkey on what we commonly refer to as "Palm Sunday."

This is significant. Because, as we've already explored, this entry into Jerusalem on a donkey was, in itself, an example of Jesus coming to his people as a nonviolent Messiah. This is why he "wept over the city" because they "did not know the things that make for peace." The people wanted a violent insurrection. Jesus wanted to bring them peace. He wept because they were impervious to his message and steadfast in their desire to shed the blood of their oppressors.

So, does it make any sense that, immediately after this scene, Jesus would stride into the Temple, fashion and whip and beat people over the head? No, it does not.

His entire mission that day was to remind his people of the way of peace. He was heartbroken that they failed to see how they might obtain his peace. He was broken inside because his people rejected him as their Prince of Peace and clung defiantly to a lust for power and a desire for armed rebellion.

Trust me, Jesus does not turn from this scene to violently attack people in the Temple. Let's take a closer look at what it actually says in the Gospels about this event:

> "In the temple courts [Jesus] found people selling cattle, sheep and doves, and others sitting at tables exchanging money. *So he made a whip out of cords,* and drove all from the temple courts, *both sheep and cattle;* he scattered the coins of the money changers and overturned their tables. To those who sold doves he said, "Get these out of here! Stop turning my Father's house into a market!" (John 2:14-16, emphasis mine)

Please note that it says Jesus used this whip to drive *"all of them from the temple courts, both sheep and cattle."* It does not say that Jesus used the whip to drive out any people. No human beings were whipped by Jesus. Not a single person. The whip was specifically used to drive "both sheep and cattle" out of the temple.

So, the actions taken by Jesus on that occasion are not to be interpreted as violent. They are rooted in His desire to restore God's Temple to its original purpose. He exercises His authority as God's Son to chase the animals and the moneychangers out of the place of worship, but He does not act violently towards anyone in the process. How can we be sure of this? Simply because scripture tells us explicitly that the Messiah to come would not be violent.

> "He [The Messiah] was assigned a grave with the wicked, and with the rich in his death, *though he had done no violence,* nor was any deceit in his mouth." (Isaiah 57:9, emphasis mine)

Let me be perfectly clear: If Jesus did act violently, he was not the Messiah according to the scriptures. So, that's how we know that Jesus did not use violence when He cleansed the Temple. Because if He had, then those who crucified Him would have been justified for crucifying Jesus as a violent man who assaulted innocent people in the Temple that day.

LET ME BE PERFECTLY CLEAR: IF JESUS DID ACT VIOLENTLY, HE WAS NOT THE MESSIAH ACCORDING TO THE SCRIPTURES. SO, THAT'S HOW WE KNOW THAT JESUS DID NOT USE VIOLENCE WHEN HE CLEANSED THE TEMPLE.

Yes, Jesus cleansed the Temple. He overturned tables. He chased animals out of the Temple using a whip he had fashioned. But He did all of that without doing any violence to another person.

GO BUY A SWORD?

In the midst of all of these passages where Jesus teaches us to love our enemies, there is this one scripture that really seems to turn everything on its head:

> "Then Jesus asked them, "When I sent you without purse, bag or sandals, did you lack anything?" "Nothing," they answered. He said to them, *"But now if you have a purse, take it, and also a bag; and if you don't have a sword, sell your cloak and buy one.* For I tell you that this Scripture must be fulfilled in me: 'And he was numbered with the transgressors.' For what is written about me has its fulfillment. The disciples said, *"See, Lord, here are two swords,"* and Jesus says, *"That's enough!"* (Luke 22: 35-38, emphasis mine)

So, if Jesus didn't intend for us to own or use swords—or other deadly weapons—then why did he say this? Well, here's what I think is going on. First of all we need to look closely at this passage in Luke. Notice that right after Jesus tells his disciples to buy a sword he goes on to say, *"For I tell you that this Scripture must be fulfilled in me: 'And he was numbered with the transgressors.' For what is written about me has its fulfillment."*

Right away we can see that Jesus' statement about the swords is directly related to prophecy—*"this Scripture must be fulfilled in me"*—and what is the prophecy that must be fulfilled? The one in Isaiah that says, *"And he was numbered with the transgressors."*

Was the statement about buying a sword about self-defense? Probably not. Because first of all, two swords are not "enough" to defend 13 guys against a legion of Roman soldiers, and secondly, because when Peter does use his sword in self-defense (or to protect Jesus from the soldiers) he is harshly rebuked with the verse we've already looked at, *"Put it away! Those who live by the sword shall die by the sword."*

Clearly, Jesus is not a fan of self-defense here. At least, not according to the overall context in this passage. However, he does tell the disciples that he wants them to have those two swords with them so that the prophecy about the Messiah being numbered with the transgressors may be fulfilled in Him. That's why two swords are "enough" for Jesus; to fulfill the scriptures, not to fight off a Roman legion, and certainly not to endorse war or approve physical violence.

Are we sure that Jesus only meant this in light of fulfilling the prophecies about Himself? Yes. How? Because after Peter cuts off the soldier's ear, listen to what Jesus has to say,

> "Do you think I cannot call on my Father, and he will at once put at my disposal more than twelve legions of angels? *But how then would the Scriptures be fulfilled that say it must happen in this way?"* (Matthew 26:53-54)

See? Jesus tells them to get a few swords so that the prophecy in Isaiah will be fulfilled. Then, once it's fulfilled in the Garden he makes a point of saying that this is what he had in mind in the first place. So, it's all about fulfilling the prophecies, not a statement from Jesus endorsing violence. To understand what Jesus has to say to his disciples about violence, please see all those other passages where he commands us to be like our Father in Heaven who loves and blesses everyone.

NOT PEACE BUT A SWORD?

Yet another startling and seemingly contradictory verse is found in the Gospels coming from the mouth of Jesus that appears to teach the opposite of what we've seen so far:

> "Do not suppose that I have come to bring peace to the earth. I did not come to bring peace, but a sword. For I have come to turn 'a man against his father, a daughter against her mother, a daughter-in-law against her mother-in-law—a man's enemies will be the members of his own household.'" (Matthew 10:34-36)

So, what is going on here? Is Jesus now contradicting his identity as the Prince of Peace? Is his mission not to bring peace at all but actually a sword?

Well, quite often in the Gospels, Jesus (and the Gospel authors) will use a common Hebraic figure of speech, sometimes called a "limited negative", to emphasize a point. These limited negatives are often constructed in this "Not A, but B" format. One example of this is found here:

> " ... children who were born, not of blood, nor of the will of the flesh, nor of the will of man, but of God." (John 1:13)

Now, what actually means is: "Not only A ... but also B" or, sometimes: "Not merely A ... but mostly B."

Such an idiom becomes recognizable when it would be absurd or contradictory to take an absolute-sounding statement in its absolute sense. In the example above, it would be foolish to try to use this verse to teach that the children of God are *not* born of blood or flesh. That would be ridiculous. Of course Christians are "born of blood" and "of the will of the flesh", but the phrase is meant to illustrate that we are not merely born of the flesh, but primarily—in a greater way—born of the Spirit.

Once you recognize this as a common idiom and figure of speech, you can easily understand many other verses of scripture from this same perspective.

Here are a few more examples of limited negatives:

- Verse: "Do not labor for the food which perishes, but for the food which endures to everlasting life." (John 6:27)

  Meaning: "Do not work *only* for natural sustenance, but *mainly* for your spiritual sustenance"

- Verse: "He who believes in me, believes not in me, but in him who sent me" (John 12:44)

  Meaning: "He who believes in me, believes *not only* in me, but *also* in him who sent me."

- Verse: " … for it is not you who speak, but the Spirit of your Father who speaks in you." (Matthew 10:20)

  Meaning: "It is not *only* you speaking, but it is *mainly* the Spirit of God speaking through you."

- Verse: "I did not come to bring peace, but a sword." (Matthew 10:34)

  Meaning: "I did not come *only* to bring peace, but *also* to bring a sword."

And what sort of "sword" is Jesus talking about here? Well, the context of the verse tells us that he is referring to division between father and son and brother and sister, etc. as some may accept Christ and others may reject Him as Messiah.

So, let's be very clear: This verse is not about violence. It's about how a decision to follow Christ may mean you lose some of your relationships. This is why Jesus elsewhere tells us to "count the cost" of becoming a disciple.

Hopefully this helps you to better understand Jesus and the other New Testament writers when they use language like this and not get confused in the future.

THE VIOLENT RETURN OF JESUS?

According to the book of Revelation, when Jesus returns He will bring an army and strike down His enemies in a final, bloody war at the end of time.

So, what exactly is going on in Revelation? Why do we see a picture of Jesus that looks so radically different than what we see in the Gospels? How did He go from the suffering servant who said, "Father, forgive them for they know not what they do" to the guy on a white horse with a sword coming out of his mouth and wearing a robe dipped in blood?

Let's look at Revelation Chapter 19 where most of this violent imagery is found. Especially these verses:

"I saw heaven standing open and there before me was a white horse, whose rider is called Faithful and True. With justice he judges and wages war. His eyes are like blazing fire, and on his head are many crowns. He has a name written on him that no one knows but he himself. He is dressed in a robe dipped in blood, and his name is the Word of God. The armies of heaven were following him, riding on white horses and dressed in fine linen, white and clean. Coming out of his mouth is a sharp sword with which to strike down the nations. "He will rule them with an iron scepter." He treads the winepress of the fury of the wrath of God Almighty. On his robe and on his thigh he has this name written: King of kings and Lord of lords.

"And I saw an angel standing in the sun, who cried in a loud voice to all the birds flying in midair, 'Come, gather together for the great supper of God, so that you may eat the flesh of kings, generals, and the mighty, of horses and their riders, and the flesh of all people, free and slave, great and small.'

"Then I saw the beast and the kings of the earth and their armies gathered together to wage war against the rider on the horse and his army. But the beast was captured, and with it the false prophet who had performed the signs on its behalf. With these signs he had deluded those who had received the mark of the beast and worshiped its image. The two of them were thrown alive into the fiery lake of burning sulfur. The rest were killed with the sword coming out of the mouth of the rider on the horse, and all the birds gorged themselves on their flesh." (Revelation 19:11-21)

Author and former mega-church pastor Mark Driscoll famously celebrated the gore of Revelation at one time, saying that Jesus is depicted here as *"a prize fighter with a tattoo down His leg, a sword in His hand and the commitment to make someone bleed."*[9]

For some Christians, this picture of Jesus is the one they prefer. Driscoll himself has said that he finds great comfort in this violent picture of Jesus because, *"... that is a guy I can worship. I cannot worship the hippie ... halo Christ because I cannot worship a guy I can beat up."*[10]

For those who embrace a more violent version of the Gospel, this kick-ass Jesus serves as a welcome buffer against the Jesus they appear to fear the most: The One who commands them to love their enemies and turn the other cheek.

But what is really happening here? Is Jesus suddenly a warmonger who delights in slaughtering thousands of His enemies?

What happened to the command that we should love our enemies? Are we held to a higher standard than God? Isn't the admonition to love our enemies connected to God's love for the just and the unjust? Aren't we imitating God when we do this? How then can we explain these passages in light of the Sermon on the Mount?

First of all, we have to recognize that the book of Revelation is a different genre of Biblical literature than the Gospels are. In the same way that none of us would read a fantasy novel like *The Lord of the Rings* the same way we might read a romance novel, or an autobiography, we cannot read all of the different books in the Bible the same way either.

The book of Revelation is an example of apocalyptic literature. As such, it contains certain motifs and even borrows specific metaphors from other apocalyptic sections of books like Isaiah, Jeremiah, Ezekiel and Daniel. These images and metaphors are never to be taken literally.

The original audiences for these writings did not believe that the smoke from a city that was judged by God would literally rise up forever and ever. They understood that this was hyperbole intended to illustrate that the finality of such judgement was absolute—as far as those who received that judgement were concerned.

In the Gospels, even Jesus referred to these same apocalyptic metaphors whenever he prophesied the destruction of Jerusalem and the end of the Jewish age. (See Matthew 24, Mark 13 and Luke 21)

So, if we understand that the images we read about in Revelation are not intended to be literal, that can help us on one level, but we still may wonder what exactly is going on and what is it we are supposed to glean from passages like chapter 19?

First of all, Revelation 19 shows us a picture of Jesus as one who is certainly playing the role of avenging warrior. At least at first glance. But if we look closer we'll see a few things that don't fit the model. For example, the sword is not in His hand, as Driscoll claims. It is coming out of His mouth. Why is that? Why does Jesus pull a sword out of His mouth like a magician on a carnival sideshow? Again, because this isn't meant to be taken literally. The sword that comes out of His mouth is symbolic. It tells us that the words spoken by Jesus have authority. His words hold the power of life and death.

NEXT, WE SEE THAT THE ROBE JESUS WEARS IS DIPPED IN BLOOD. BUT WE MUST KEEP IN MIND THAT THIS BLOOD IS NOT THE BLOOD OF HIS ENEMIES. IT IS HIS OWN BLOOD.

Next, we see that the robe Jesus wears is dipped in blood. But we must keep in mind that this blood is not the blood of His enemies. *It is His own blood.* Jesus has already suffered for the sins of the entire world.

Still, we have to admit that the imagery near the end of the chapter is quite gruesome. Birds are called to gorge themselves on the flesh of the slain. But, again, we have to remember that the connection between the apocalyptic hyperbole and the actual fulfillment is not the same thing.

For example, when God prophesied against Egypt in Isaiah 19, we read that God will be seen *"riding on a swift cloud"* (v.1) as He comes to judge that nation. This is not a literal event. God is not saddling up a cloud and riding into battle against Egypt. The fulfillment of that image is when the armies of an invading nation ride into battle against Egypt and destroy her cities. In other words, these fantastic images of God (or Jesus) riding into battle against the people of the earth to do battle with them is fulfilled when the armies of other nations rise up and attack. There is always a practical fulfillment to these sorts of prophesies, as we see whenever God's prophets proclaim judgment on nations using these kinds of apocalyptic hyperbole.

In Ezekiel 39 when God prophesies against Assyria (or Gog) He says *"I will give you to the birds of prey of every sort and the beasts of the field to be devoured."* (v.4) This is the exact same apocalyptic hyperbole used in Revelation 19 to describe the fate of those who will be judged by the words spoken by Jesus against those who reject Him as their King.

Simply put, this section of Revelation—like most of the book—is about the destruction of Jerusalem in AD 70 and the end of the age (not the end of the world). The author of Revelation borrows violent apocalyptic hyperbole found in the Old Covenant scriptures to illustrate this event. He expresses it in dramatic, yes even violent, metaphorical terminology. But if we boil everything down, all that is really happening in Revelation 19 is that Jesus, who is the Judge, speaks life to those who love Him and those who reject that life receive the penalty of death.

But, please understand, Jesus takes no pleasure in the death of anyone. Not even those who reject Him. His love for you is the same as His love for Hitler. That is to say: enough to die for both of you and to extend to everyone the same mercy, grace and forgiveness.

So, what's on display here—in Apocalyptic terms—is what happened to the Jewish people after they rejected Jesus's call to "metanoia"—literally "to change their minds"—and turn away from their desire to violently overthrow the Roman occupation.

What's confusing to us is that it's Jesus who is seen riding the horse and bringing the destruction, but we know that it wasn't Jesus who destroyed the Temple and ended the daily sacrifice, it was the Roman army. However, there is a sense in which it was Jesus if you take the perspective that he warned his people this was coming and urged them to walk another path—the way that makes for peace—and when they rejected him, his prophecy about where that violent path would take them came to fruition.

There's a sense in which the destruction of Jerusalem in AD 70 by the Romans was a vindication of Jesus's ministry. In other words, once this event took place exactly as he said it would in his Olivet Discourse, everyone knew that Jesus was truly the Messiah that was sent from God in those last days. Placing Jesus on the white horse that comes down from the sky is consistent with all those other Old Testament passages where God comes to bring judgment on Edom, and Egypt, and yes, even Jerusalem. Not because Jesus is the one doing the killing, but to connect the warnings he gave them with the fulfillment of the prophetic word.

NO REBUKE TO SOLDIERS?

Sometimes, the naysayers will point to examples in the Gospels where Jesus interacted with Roman soldiers and centurions and didn't rebuke them for their military service. (See Matthew 8:5-13)

First of all, let's keep in mind that this logic leads to some uncomfortable conclusions if applied to other scenarios in the life of Jesus. For example, if what we're supposed to understand by Jesus's lack of rebuke to the centurion is that Jesus was in favor of military service or participation in violent conflict, what are we to say about those times when Jesus encounters known prostitutes and says nothing to them about their chosen profession? Does his silence in those cases prove that Jesus fully endorsed prostitution? Obviously, not. So, the fact that Jesus doesn't directly admonish the centurion is no more a sign of his approval of the man's lifestyle than is his silence towards prostitutes.

Still, there are those who argue that, if Jesus was so anti-violence, why didn't he take these encounters with soldiers as opportunities to say so?

Well, I'd like to point out that Jesus has already "said so" in a half-dozen other places in the Gospels. So, we shouldn't need him to offer yet another lesson in nonviolence for us to "get it." But, more than that, the thing we need to keep in mind is that Jesus never rebuked non-believers, or Gentiles, or "sinners" in his ministry. He always reserved the public rebuke for members of the professional religious elite.

So, when Jesus interacts with a Roman centurion, he knows this man is not seeking to become one of his disciples. See, it's only to his disciples that Jesus gave his Sermon on the Mount, and it's only to the people of Israel that he presents this Gospel message of loving their enemies. In fact, it's precisely because his own people are so hell-bent on a violent rebellion against the Roman Empire that Jesus directly confronts them about it. He tries to show them that this path of insurrection will only end in the destruction of their Temple, their priesthood, their daily sacrifice and their way of life. He offers them another path that leads to life; one that involves loving their Roman occupiers and disarming them with love. So, that's why we don't see him correcting the Roman soldiers, because they're not the ones he was called to proclaim the Kingdom of God to. The Romans were not following him. But, the Jewish people were looking for a Messiah; they were searching for someone to show them the way out of their situation. Sadly, when he shows up and offers them the only way that works, they rejected this message of enemy love and put him to death.

No, Jesus does not take the time to rebuke the Roman soldier—who is not his disciple—for being a soldier. But, what Jesus *does* do is to commend the soldier for his faith, extending mercy to him and even healing his servant; something that was an example to his own people for how they should also respond to their Roman occupiers, with mercy and grace. In other words, Jesus models for his disciples and his people what it looks like to bless those who curse you, turn the other cheek and love your enemies. It's an object lesson for them, and for us, to follow in our quest to embody the love of Christ to everyone around us.

RETHINKING PARADIGMS

At the very end of this exchange between Jesus and the Roman centurion in Matthew 8:5-13, Jesus affirms the great faith of his Gentile soldier and then says something fairly astounding:

> "I say to you that many will come from the east and the west, and will take their places at the feast with Abraham, Isaac and Jacob in the kingdom of heaven. But the subjects of the kingdom will be thrown outside, into the darkness, where there will be weeping and gnashing of teeth." (v.11-2)

For the longest time, I have always read this verse as saying that those who enter the Kingdom from the east and the west—meaning peoples from many tongues, tribes and nations—will get to enjoy this wonderful opportunity to "take their places at the feast … in the Kingdom." But, I've always read that second verse as it it's warning us that the "sinners" and those outside the Kingdom will suffer and be cast into outer "darkness where there will be weeping and gnashing of teeth." But, that is not what Jesus says at all. Go ahead and re-read that final verse and you'll notice something fairly startling: "But the subjects of the Kingdom will be thrown outside into the darkness where there will be weeping and gnashing of teeth." Yes, that's not a typo. Jesus says that it's the "subjects of the Kingdom", (or the "heirs" or "sons" of the Kingdom), who are going to be cast into the darkness where there is weeping and gnashing of teeth, not the "sinners" or the "unbelievers."

What? How can this be? A close look at other translations confirm this reading. In the new translation of the New Testament by David Bentley Hart, the verse reads this way:

> "But the sons of the Kingdom will be thrown out into the darkness outside; there will be weeping and grinding of teeth there." (Matt. 8:12, DBH)

Honestly, I don't know how many years of my life have gone by as I've read and re-read that verse, probably hundreds of times, and never once noticed what Jesus was actually saying. I suppose my brain just flipped these words around in my head so that I understood it to be saying what I expected it to say: that the sinners would be those cast into darkness, that unbelievers would suffer the weeping and the gnashing of teeth, not us.

So, now that we can see what the words are *saying*, how can we better understand what those words *mean*?

I think the clue may be found in the ways we've been conditioned to understand some of Jesus's parables. Namely, the ones where we've assumed that God was the King who cast the guest at the wedding banquet out into the darkness for not wearing the proper wedding garment, or that God was the Master who rebuked his servant for not turning his one talent into more talents. Perhaps we should reinvestigate those parables to see what we've been missing and search for better ways to understand this teaching in context.

THE PARABLE OF THE WEDDING BANQUET

All my life I've read certain parables from Jesus as if the King or the Master character must be God, and the one who gets beaten, tortured and cast outside into the darkness must be those "sinners" who reject the Gospel. Now, I'm not so sure.

Let's try to reexamine a few of those parables with this new paradigm we've discovered in Matthew 8:12 and see if there's something we're missing.

In the Parable of the Wedding Feast, found in Matthew 22:1-14, Jesus tells the story of a King who prepared a wedding banquet for his son. He sends his servants out to invite people to attend, but they refuse. He sends them out again and they either ignore the invitation, or they seize his servants, beat them, and kill them. This enrages the King who sends his army to "destroy those murderers and burn their city." (v.7) Then, he tells his servants to go out into the streets and "gather all the people they can find; the bad as well as the good" (v.10) and this fills up the wedding hall. So far, so good. But then the King notices one man who is not wearing the proper attire for the banquet, the King angrily confronts the man, and "the man was speechless." (v.12) That's when the King orders his servants to "tie him hand and foot and throw him outside, into the darkness, where there will be weeping and gnashing of teeth." (v.13)

First of all, we probably tend to misread this parable as if the King is God. Why? Because he wants to "prepare a wedding banquet for his son" and that sounds a lot like the "Wedding Feast of the Lamb" spoken of in Revelation and elsewhere. Surely, this must be a clue for us to follow. Especially when paired with the note that the King's servants were beaten and killed by those he invited. That totally sounds like a reference to the way the Jewish people treated the prophets who came before Jesus, doesn't it? We even hear Jesus say exactly this in Matthew 5:11-13. Then another apparent reference to God comes when he instructs his servants to "go out into the streets and gather all the people they could find … both bad and good … " That really sounds like God's heart to include everyone, doesn't it?

So, where is the first hint that this King is not God, or that the wedding feast is not the Wedding Feast of the Lamb? I believe it's when the King turns to notice the man who doesn't have on the right wedding garments and responds in anger rather than compassion. I mean, could you really see Jesus turning to attack a man in the crowd who couldn't afford nice enough clothing for the royal party? Hopefully not. Then, we see that the man's response to the angry King is simply this: "the man was speechless." Can we think of another example where an angry ruler threatens someone who's only response is to be as silent as a lamb? Yes, of course we can. First, in Isaiah 53:7-9 where we read:

> "He was oppressed and he was afflicted, yet he did not open his mouth; like a lamb that is led to slaughter, and like a sheep that is silent before its shearers, so he did not open his mouth."

This Messianic passage is affirmed in the trial of Jesus just before his crucifixion where we read that Jesus, after being accused by false witnesses is asked by the High Priest, *"Do you make no answer, for what these men are testifying against you?" And Jesus was silent. (Matt. 26:62-63)* Later that same morning, when Jesus stands before Pilate he is asked, *"Do you make no answer? See how many charges they bring against you." But Jesus made no further answer, so that Pilate was amazed." (Mark 15:4-5).* Then, after being sent to Herod we read that *"Herod … questioned him at some length, but he [Jesus] answered him nothing" (Luke 23:9)*

Now we can see a parallel between this unnamed wedding guest and Jesus. But, there's more. If the King in this parable is not God, then who is he? Might it be the ruler of the Empire that was oppressing the Jewish people at that time? If so, then it would make sense that Jesus's response would be to refuse to participate in this ceremony. And, isn't this exactly what happens to Jesus when he opposes both the religious and political powers of his day? They seize him, bind him, beat him, and then take him outside the city walls where he is crucified on a Roman cross.

Several other New Testament scholars have argued that this alternate reading of the parable is based on historical events that took place in Jerusalem around the same time that Jesus spoke these words. For example, King Herod, who ruled Jerusalem at this time, fits the description of the ruler in this parable to a tee.

As Biblical scholar Marty Aiken argues:

> "[In] the story of Herod the Great we find a story remarkably similar to the events, and certainly the logic, of the parable. We find a hint almost immediately of mimetic tension among the rulers of Jerusalem ... Herod's situation ... is actually even more analogous, in fact it begins to become identical to, the situation of the king in the parable.

> "Is there anything in Jesus' remarks about the parable's king that would suggest to the audience that Jesus was in fact referring to the king the priests acknowledge and serve? ... Was there a wedding in the history of the Herodian dynasty that had such real and/or symbolic importance that it would continue to be associated with any member of the Herodian dynasty, up to and including here this day at the Temple? If so, would it jump off the page at the audience, so to speak?

> " ... Herod [was] engaged to, but not yet married to, the grand-daughter of the high priest Hyrcanus. If Herod can consummate this marriage he will have associated with himself and bestowed upon his son the legitimacy and renown of the Hasmonean royal line. By the same token, he has been named a king but he has never sat on his throne, leaving his kingship unconsummated as well.

> "[in this parable], Jesus tells us of a king obsessed with completing a wedding in a wedding hall filled with what are essentially

prisoners for guests while a city burns behind them. Parable and history have gone from paralleling each other to intersecting with each other at a final common denominator of undifferentiated violence seeking a way to restrain itself.

"One of my fundamental points is that the parable is also faithful to an 'anecdotal history' and that the audience of the parable will experience recognizable anecdotes in the events of the parable. I also suggest that the audience will be pre-loaded to look for references to Herod in references to a king, particularly since they anticipate Jesus' speech is a preface to a confrontation ... there is a structural and a "spiritual" similarity between Herod's entreaty to the rulers of Jerusalem and the wedding banquet the king proposes in the parable.

"I think it very likely that Herod would come to mind, and I also think it very likely that his marriage on the eve of the battle by which he conquered Jerusalem would be a part of the popular imagination. In fact, given the parable's immediate reference to a king and a wedding banquet, the thought of Herod's pre-battle marriage would be more likely to have been the first association anyone made with the parable's wedding banquet setting."[11]

So, we have historical and scriptural reasons for accepting the notion that this parable reflects a picture of a violent king and a suffering servant who refuses to bow to the ruler's authority and becomes the object of the king's wrath. In this reading, the one who is bound hand and foot and cast outside into the darkness is Jesus, not an unrepentant sinner.

This new way of seeing allows us to see what Jesus may be alluding to in the passage where he says that it's "*the sons of the Kingdom [who] will be thrown out into the darkness ... [where] there will be weeping and grinding of teeth there.*" (Matt. 8:12, *DBH*) If so, then this phrase is a reference to how the rulers of this age treated Jesus, and not a reference to how God will respond to the unrighteous.

Let's examine another parable to see if it fits this same paradigm.

THE PARABLE OF THE TALENTS

In the parable of the talents, Jesus tells us about another ruler—a Master of great wealth who owns slaves—and his desire to build wealth for himself while he is away. He gives 5 talents to one servant, 2 to another and 1 to yet another of his slaves. When he returns, he's elated to find that the one with 5 talents has doubled his money, so he rewards him. His second servant also doubled his money and receives his reward, but the last servant has buried his talent in the ground and simply gives back to the Master what belongs to the Master, and nothing more. For this, the servant is *"cast ... into the outer darkness where there will be weeping and gnashing of teeth."* (Matt. 25:14-30)

Once again, there are signs near the beginning of the parable that the Master is an analog for God or even perhaps Christ himself; He's called "Lord", he goes away for a long time and then suddenly returns to settle accounts, and he rewards the good servants by saying "well done, good and faithful servant ... enter into the joy of your lord." (v. 23) All of that sure sounds like we're dealing with God in this parable, doesn't it? But, let's keep in mind that part of what Jesus came to do was to correct our misunderstandings about who God was and what God was like. Prior to the coming of Jesus, the Jewish people certainly saw God as fitting the description of both the King in the previous parable and the Master in this one. But, Jesus flips their perspectives upside down and halfway through these stories the tables are turned. It's not God who is the harsh and angry King. It's God, or Christ, as the wedding guest who can't afford nice clothes and says nothing as he's beaten and cast outside into the darkness. It's not God who is the greedy, wrathful slave owner. It's God, or Christ, as the one servant who has the courage to refuse to participate in the economic system of oppression where one man collects great wealth at the expense of slave labor.

When the servant in this parable of the talents gives back to the Master what belongs to the Master (v. 25), it should remind us of something Jesus said when asked about paying taxes to the Roman Empire: "Give to Caesar what is Caesar's and to God what is God's." (Luke 20:25) And, again, isn't this parable a picture of exactly what happened to Jesus when he condemned the oppressive taxation of widows in Luke 20:45-47 and 21:1-4? Isn't this what happens to Jesus when he dares to upset the lucrative economic structure of the moneychangers in the temple?

Perhaps we should re-read this parable in light of these ideas and then we might see that Jesus is the one who refuses to take part in the oppressive system where Masters exploit their slaves for profit. Maybe then we could see how Jesus mirrors the servant who merely gives back to the rulers of this age what is theirs without enriching them in the process.

If we're on the right track, then these parables provide clear pictures of how Jesus is both the unclothed wedding guest and the one-talent servant who suffer the violence and wrath of the oppressive political and religious systems; being beaten, tortured and cast into outer darkness where there is weeping and gnashing of teeth.

We already known that Jesus was taken by the Kings, and the Masters, in his day and crucified outside the city walls in disgrace. How else are we to understand these parables, especially if we look for Jesus in them?

Honestly, I think it's very possible that even the disciples themselves may have understood these parables in the traditional way, prior to the crucifixion of Jesus, and then another way afterwards. In other words, our assumptions about what God is like may color our perceptions more than realize. If we take the "Flat Bible" approach, for example, we may tend to see God as the wrathful, jealous king and master who has no tolerance for anyone who dares defy him. But, if we take a "Jesus-Centric" view of God, we may suddenly discover that it's inconsistent with the character of Christ to view God as the wrathful king or the harsh slave-owner. Instead, we may

IF WE TAKE A "JESUS-CENTRIC" VIEW OF GOD, WE MAY SUDDENLY DISCOVER THAT IT'S INCONSISTENT WITH THE CHARACTER OF CHRIST TO VIEW GOD AS THE WRATHFUL KING OR THE HARSH SLAVE-OWNER.

notice how much like Jesus those unfortunate servants and wedding guests were who did not submit to the authority of those men, but instead subversively resisted those powers and paid the ultimate price for doing so.

I don't know about you, but I'm inclined to accept the notion that this must be what Jesus means when he says in Matthew 8:12 that *"the sons of the Kingdom will be thrown outside, into the darkness where there will be weeping and gnashing of teeth."* It is an accurate picture of what happens to him at his crucifixion, and a vivid reminder that those who follow his example might expect similar results.

As Jesus affirms:

"If the world hates you, you know that it hated Me before it hated you. If you were of the world, the world would love its own. Yet because you are not of the world, but I chose you out of the world, therefore the world hates you. Remember the word that I said to you, 'A servant is not greater than his master.' If they persecuted Me, they will also persecute you. If they kept My word, they will keep yours also." (John 15:18-20)

In other words, if Jesus was the one whom the angry king tortured for not dressing the part, and also the one whom the harsh slave master cast out into the darkness for not increasing his wealth, then we might also expect to receive the same treatment ourselves as "sons of the Kingdom."

So, when it comes to those verses that seem to celebrate violence, it always pays to take another look and to refocus our attention on where we see Jesus in the story, without falling back on our assumptions about God being wrathful, angry or violent. When we do, we often discover new concepts that would otherwise remain hidden from our understanding.

For now, let's turn our attention away from the scriptural support for enemy-love and take a look at the stark contrast between Biblical violence and Christlike love.

CHAPTER 4

BIBLICAL VIOLENCE OR CHRISTLIKE LOVE?

"For Jesus, there are no countries to be conquered, no ideologies to be imposed, no people to be dominated. There are only children, women and men to be loved."

— HENRI NOUWEN

One of the reasons why so many Christians are confused by the notion of Christian nonviolence is because the Bible seems to advocate for war on numerous occasions. So, to them, warfare and violence are "Biblical" concepts and, therefore, should not be rejected. However, what they misunderstand is the difference between something that is "Biblical" and something that is "Christlike." The two are not synonymous. For example, these are all "Biblical" ideas: Genocide, Patriarchy, Polygamy, Slavery, and—as we've already said—War. But, none of those ideas are "Christlike." Here's why: Jesus is the Messiah who was foretold to come and teach us a new path that would lead us to peace. This path was not found in Moses, nor was it taught by Elijah, or Daniel, or King David. In fact, all of those men were suffering from the same problem: they did not know Christ. But, once Christ comes, our eyes can be opened to this new path and we can catch glimpses of it in these pre-Christian texts if we are looking carefully.

WHAT THIS MEANS IS THAT, PRIOR TO THE COMING OF CHRIST, NO ONE—NOT MOSES, NOT ISAIAH, NOT DANIEL, NOT ELIJAH, NOR ANY OTHER HUMAN AUTHOR OF SCRIPTURE— EVER SAW GOD CLEARLY.

This revelation is, I believe, the key to unlocking the contradictions that abound between the Old Covenant and the New Covenant Scriptures. For me, the recognition of a "Jesus-Centric" approach to the Bible was a revolutionary one. Suddenly, I could see where Jesus corrected prior misunderstandings about who God was and what God was like. Because, as the Gospel of John emphatically and quite shockingly proclaims:

> "No one has ever seen God at any time, except for the Son of God who came to make Him known to us." (John 1:18)

What this means is that, prior to the coming of Christ, no one—not Moses, not Isaiah, not Daniel, not Elijah, nor any other human author of scripture—ever saw God clearly. It was only when Jesus came that we could, finally, see who God actually was and what God was really like. This is exactly the implication of the statement repeated over and over by Jesus: "If you've seen me, you've seen the Father." Because, only Jesus shows us the heart, mind, character and posture of God towards humanity.

It also means that, without Jesus, we have no clear pictures of God to look at. It means that our previous assumptions about God were wrong. This is entirely why it was even necessary for Jesus to come—to make the Father known to us! Why? Because we were unclear about God prior to his coming. This is why the Apostle Paul says:

" … For to this day the same veil remains when the old covenant is read. It has not been removed, because only in Christ is the veil removed." (2 Cor. 3:14)

In other words, if you read the Old Covenant scriptures without first knowing Jesus, you are guaranteed to get it wrong. However, if you abide in Christ as Christ abides in you and you learn to recognize the character of Jesus, then—and only then—will you have discernment to see and hear the voice of the Father as revealed in Christ.[12]

For many of us, even when we start to approach the Scriptures thru this lens of Christ, we are still often tempted to appeal to what we might call "common sense" when it comes to questions of violence or war.

Right away, I'd want to caution those who want to appeal to such common sense thinking by saying that, if the way of Jesus was based on common sense, there would have been no need for him to come to us. In other words, if what we needed was just common sense, then God would have sent us a logic teacher, or a philosopher, rather than a Messiah who would teach us a new way to think, and an uncommon way to live.

The Gospel that Jesus preached was, and is, a revolutionary "upside down" approach to life. What's down is up, the first are last, the one's who humble themselves are exalted, the greatest is the lowest servant, those who lose their lives find true, everlasting life, even as they die daily.

Does any of that sound to you like "common sense"? Obviously, not. Instead, Jesus offers us a way that is otherwise unknown and unheard of. In fact, even when we *do* see this new path, it can look entirely strange and perhaps even a bit ridiculous to our minds.

Still, our options are to ignore the way of Jesus—because it just seems at odds with what we might call common sense—or we reach a point where we've tried everything else we can think of and find ourselves at a place where we're willing to try anything—even something so upside down and backwards from anything else we've ever heard of before—if it means finding the path that leads us to life, and peace, and joy, as we abide in the presence of God.

Until we reach this point in our lives, we will most likely continue to fall back on "common sense" and rationalize that "in the real world" we must sometimes resort to violence to fight evil, or to rescue the weak or the powerless. But there are hundreds of examples throughout history where creative nonviolent resistance has proven itself to be even more effective than the use of violence. Even in what many would call the ultimate "Just War"—World War II—there are numerous examples of nonviolence working marvelously to thwart the Nazis and their tactics.

WHEN IT COMES TO THE QUESTION OF JUST WAR VERSUS NONVIOLENT ENEMY LOVE, IT'S QUITE CLEAR THAT ONLY ONE OF THOSE APPROACHES ACTUALLY WORKS IN THE REAL WORLD, AND THAT IS THE PATH OF NONVIOLENCE.

Not to mention all the other examples throughout history—in both national and personal conflicts—where nonviolence has defeated tyrants, disarmed the aggressors, and won freedom for the oppressed.

Yes, as we've also seen, there are times when those who respond with nonviolence are arrested, beaten, injured, tortured and even killed. But, even in those cases, their nonviolent resistance has served as an example of Christlike love in action, inspiring thousands to reconsider the peaceful way of Jesus.

When it comes to the question of Just War versus Nonviolent Enemy Love, it's quite clear that only one of those approaches actually works in the real world, and that is the path of nonviolence. As theologian and historian David Bercot explains:

"Sure, the Just War position sounds good on paper, but it's a fantasy position. The Just War theory has never been used to stop any war that I know of ... nor has there ever been a war where all or most Christians refused to participate because they believed the war was unjust. The simple truth is, in every war, Christians on all sides have said, 'we're fighting for a just cause ... '" Under this philosophy, every war in the Middle Ages was a Just War. Even when Christians and the Church were in charge, Pope's declared all wars were just, including the Crusades and the invasion of England by the Norman's. In contrast, we've had more peace in Europe over these last 70 years—where people have largely given up on Christianity—than we ever did during all those centuries when Christianity was in power there ... [Just War theory] just doesn't work in real life. People always come up with their justification and so they always go to war."[13]

In other words, the Just War theory essentially adds up to this: No matter how you look at it, it's just war, plain and simple.

Over the last 1,700 years or so, Christians have largely turned—not to Jesus—but to the Old Testament to justify going to war. They've listened, not to Jesus, but to Ambrose, and Augustine, and Luther, when it comes to using violence.

I love how my friend Rob Grayson describes this process, by asking us to stop and ask ourselves a few probing questions, like:

"How many times down the centuries have Christians indulged in excessive peace-making, non-violence and mercy and then projected that peaceful image onto God as justification for their peace-filled worldview? Conversely, how many times have Christians down the centuries indulged in excessive aggression, violence and vengeance and then projected that onto God as justification for their violent ways?

"As human beings, we are not at much risk of spontaneously being too nice, kind, loving, compassionate and non-violent. Left unchecked, however, we are very likely to spontaneously be unpleasant, unkind, unloving, merciless and violent.

"So when you see someone insisting that violence is part of God's nature, ask yourself how likely it is that they are projecting their own violent human tendencies onto God, just as some of the biblical writers did.

"And when you see someone trying to read the Bible discerningly so as to discover the all-forgiving, enemy-loving, non-violent God, consider the possibility that they have actually dared to come to terms with their own violence and to see that God, by contrast, is absolutely non-violent."[14]

The way of Jesus is not our way. The path of peace is not our default. We must learn to walk in this path. It will involve a rewiring of our brains, and a transformation of our hearts. The first step is to admit that all of our previous ways of dealing with evil and responding to conflict have failed miserably.

WAR IS OUR WORST IDEA. IT'S NOT A SOLUTION TO THE PROBLEM OF EVIL.

War is our worst idea. It's not a solution to the problem of evil. In many ways, it *is* the evil. This internal violence is what we must ask Jesus to cast out of us, like the Legion of demons that possessed the wild man who lived among the tombs of the dead, before we can even begin to walk the path of peace.

In our next chapter, let's take a look at the more practical applications of nonviolent resistance. After all, just because something may make sense on paper, it doesn't necessarily follow that the same ideas will actually work in the real world.

CHAPTER 5

NONVIOLENCE: DOES IT WORK?

"Lord, if I thought you were listening, I'd pray for this above all: that any church set up in your name should remain poor, and powerless, and modest. That it should wield no authority except that of love. That it should never cast anyone out. That it should own no property and make no laws. That it should not condemn, but only forgive. That it should be not like a palace with marble walls and polished floors, and guards standing at the door, but like a tree with its roots deep in the soil, that shelters every kind of bird and beast and gives blossom in the spring and shade in the hot sun and fruit in the season, and in time gives up its good sound wood for the carpenter; but that sheds many thousands of seeds so that new trees can grow in its place."

— PHILIP PULLMAN[15]

In this ongoing conversation between Christians about how to follow those "Love your enemy" commands that Jesus spoke over us, there's always this lingering question that falls somewhere between "Did Jesus really mean that?" and "Is it really possible to do this?" and that question is: "But, does this nonviolence thing even work?"

While this is a good question to ask ourselves before we venture out into Enemy-Loving territory, it's also one of the many deflections that we use to postpone our practice of it. Still, we need to take some time to explore this with as much honesty and sincerity as we can. After all, once we know the answer to this question, we may finally find ourselves ready to walk the path that Jesus invites us to walk.

So, does it work? Can nonviolence really resolve our conflicts? If so, then why didn't it work on Hitler or the Nazis? Why didn't nonviolence stop all the other genocides throughout history? Why is it that war—and only war—has ever worked to overthrow oppressive governments, end brutal dictatorships and free the prisoners of tyranny?

THE SHORT ANSWER IS THAT NONVIOLENCE HASN'T WORKED TO STOP ALL THOSE INJUSTICES IN OUR PAST FOR ONE SIMPLE REASON: NO ONE TRIED IT.

The short answer is that nonviolence hasn't worked to stop all those injustices in our past for one simple reason: No one tried it. But, that answer isn't completely accurate. The truth is that there have been pockets of nonviolent resistance used in certain places by select people in response to oppressive regimes, and guess what? In almost every case it worked. But don't take my word for it.

In his book *Engaging the Powers*, Walter Wink records how the Nazi's had no way of dealing with those who responded to their aggression with non-violent resistance. As he points out:

> "B.H. Liddell-Hart, widely acknowledged as the foremost military writer of our times, discovered in his interrogation of Nazi generals after World War II that they had little trouble dealing with violent resistance except in mountainous areas of Russia and the Balkins, or where advancing armies were close. But they expressed complete inability to cope with nonviolence as practiced in Denmark, Holland, Norway, and, to a lesser extent, in France and Belgium.

"'They were experts in violence, and had been trained to cope with opponents who used that method. But other forms of resistance baffled them. They were relieved when nonviolence was mixed with guerilla operations, which made it easier to combine suppressive action against both at the same time.'

"The generals found friendly noncompliance more frustrating than any other form of resistance, and had no effective means to counter it. 'If practiced with a cheerful smile and an air of well-meaning mistake, due to incomprehension or clumsiness, it becomes even more baffling … This subtle kind of resistance cannot really be dealt with in terms of force: indeed, nothing can deal with it. There is really no answer to such go-slow tactics."

So, when the Nazi war machine was met with an intentional, organized nonviolent resistance, they had no grid for how to respond. As we said, quite often the assumed "failure" of nonviolence is simply that it is so seldom attempted.

Strikingly enough, however, there *were* more nonviolent movements to oppose the spread of Nazism during World War 2 than most of us have ever been told about. Perhaps because such examples do not support our accepted narrative of the power of redemptive violence. Whatever the case, there are plenty of cases to examine and a variety of nonviolent responses to consider. As historian George Paxton details:

"The methods used in the various campaigns [against the Nazis] were very diverse such as marches, wearing symbols of resistance, private and public letters of protest, refusing to be conscripted for work, resigning from professional bodies taken over by the Nazis, hiding Jews, helping Jews escape, listening to BBC radio broadcasts, producing underground newspapers, collecting funds for resistance, deliberate slow working and many more."[16]

" … the White Rose group in Germany is one of the most impressive examples. Set up mainly by students at the University of Munich and including a brother and sister, Hans and Sophie

Scholl, the group produced leaflets attacking the immoral nature of the Nazi regime and also the likelihood of its failure. Leaflets were printed secretly then posted out to individuals and left in public places. Groups were also started in other German towns and leaflets were transported by a resister by train in a suitcase.

"But due to a careless act when Hans and Sophie were distributing leaflets at their university, they were arrested, interrogated, quickly tried and executed. This was followed by other arrests, executions and imprisonments. While their resistance was a failure in that the revolt of students they hoped to trigger did not occur, knowledge of their courageous acts spread widely in Germany and indeed abroad.

"A contrasting successful resistance was the rescue of Jews, mainly children, by the villagers of Chambon-sur-Lignon on a high plateau south-west of Lyons in France. This village [and others in the region] became a hide-out for those escaping the Nazis and became a centre of safety, particularly for children. The inspiration for this action came from the Protestant pastor and his wife, André and Magda Trocmé. André was an in-comer from the north-east of France and a pacifist and his actions were a product of his Christian belief which influenced also the nature of the resistance. Thus he did not deny that Jews were hidden in the village and surrounding farms but refused to tell the police where they were hidden. André survived the occupation, although imprisoned for a time, and several thousand Jews and others hidden there survived until liberation.

"There are detailed studies of these two cases published but many more have not been studied in detail and indeed no doubt some actions have been lost to history.

"Although there were only about 8,000 Jews in Denmark almost all of them survived."[17]

As inspiring as these examples are, Paxton shares several other examples from all over Europe:

"One of the most outstanding successes of resistance was the rescue of the Danish Jews. *Denmark* was treated relatively mildly by the Germans in part because the Danes were willing to supply Germany with agricultural produce. Their own government was allowed considerable independence for a while although the relationship soured eventually and the Germans took over.

"The local German administration was then ordered to round up the Jews for deportation to Germany. But at the German embassy was an attaché, Georg Duckwitz, who contacted a leading Danish politician to tell him when the round-up was to take place. He, in turn, informed the Chief Rabbi who passed the word to the Jews, while non-Jewish friends hid Jews and then transported them to the coast where boats were hired to take them to neutral Sweden. Although there were only about 8,000 Jews in Denmark almost all of them survived, even the few hundred who were captured and sent to Germany were not sent to the death camps as had been promised to SS General Werner Best, the German head of government in Denmark.

"*In the Netherlands*, an attempt to conscript former Dutch soldiers who had been disarmed by the Germans was met by the largest strike in the occupied countries. It began in mines and factories and spread until it involved half a million people who took to the streets. In response, more than 100 people were executed but far fewer former soldiers enrolled than the Germans wanted.

"*In Belgium,* students and staff at the University of Brussels protested at the employment of Nazi staff and then organized teaching underground.

"*In the Netherlands and Norway* the Germans failed to bring the doctors' professional associations under their control due to non-cooperation by the doctors.

"Opposition in Germany, particularly by Catholics, forced the stopping of the 'euthanasia' program, although many had been murdered before it was abandoned."[18]

So, while World War 2 is often the "go-to" environment for testing the efficacy of nonviolence, there are several other examples of how tyrants have been deposed in numerous places without bloodshed. For example, oppressive regimes have been removed by nonviolent action in Russia (Gorbachev, 1991), Poland (Jaruzelski, 1989), Hungary (Kadar, 1989), Serbia (Milosevic, 2000), Philippines (Marcos, 1986), Chile (Pinochet, 1988), Czechoslovakia (Dubeck, 1968), Greece (Karamanlis, 1995), Slovenia (Kucan, 1991), and Nepal (Birendra, 1990), to name just a few.

One of the most fascinating examples of how an organized nonviolent resistance can inspire a nation and provide a catalyst for lasting transformation is what happened in the West African Republic of Liberia in 2003. This was when social worker Leymah Gbowee started a peace movement comprised of ordinary women—both Muslims and Christians—who gathered to sit, sing and pray together in protest of their nation's bloody civil war. Armed with only their courage, their prayers and their desire for peace, these women, who numbered over 3,000 strong, disrupted the daily routine and caught the attention of their media, their nation and their leaders until their President eventually agreed to a meeting. There, Liberian President Charles Taylor was forced to agree to attend peace talks in Ghana. Once he arrived in Ghana, President Taylor was met with a delegation of women—also led by Leymah Gbowee—who continued to apply pressure for a peace agreement, and even staged a silent protest outside of the Presidential Palace. Eventually, after a 14-year-long civil war, a peace agreement was reached.[19]

MORE PROOF

Need more examples? Okay, then. Here we go.

In her book, *Why Civil Resistance Works: Non-Violence in the Past and Future*, author Erica Chenoweth's research on the viability of non-violence as an effective tool in the face of real-world violence and oppression is impeccable and compelling. As she documents, nonviolent resistance has a more effective track record for success than violent insurgency. Looking at over 300 cases where nonviolence was employed she found—contrary to her own expectations and that of the literature at the time—that "nonviolent campaigns were almost were almost twice as successful as violent insurgencies, from 1900 to 2006 … and also more than twice as likely to achieve at least partial success, which is … significant concessions, for instance where they force the dictator to hold real, true, competitive elections … and violent campaigns are more than twice as likely to fail."[20]

Another finding that surprised Chenoweth was how nonviolent campaigns gradually increased in frequency over time. "So, [according to her research], violent campaigns are becoming an increasingly ineffective method of [resolving] conflict, whereas nonviolent resistance is becoming increasingly effective over time."[21]

Because of these findings, Chenoweth decided to study why civil resistance succeeded so often relative to armed insurgency. After studying specific cases in detail, what she found was that nonviolent campaigns were generally far better at attracting diverse, and large numbers of participants that sustain momentum over time, relative to armed campaigns. Therefore:

> " … the source of success for most non-State actors is people power … and nonviolent campaigns are much better at sustaining people power and accessing points of power within a society based on the composition of their membership. So, the strategy of armed insurgency is to get as many people as you can with as many guns as you can to take on the State opponent. You don't always take it on directly by going to the battlefield. Sometimes you do sabotage or assassinations, you build a network of sympathizers and supporters. But you're fighting the regime and your

object is to take them down from the center to corrode their capacity to maintain power. This is a very difficult way to win. The strategy of nonviolent resistance is not to actually confront the State, or the regime elites, at the top. Instead, the strategy is to leverage people power to pull the pillars that support that regime at the top away from it. In other words, every regime has people it needs to rely on to maintain power. Whether these are economic elites, business elites, security forces, police, civilian bureaucrats, state media, etc., it needs their active obedience and cooperation to maintain power. The power of civil resistance adheres from its ability to start disrupting the ability and willingness for those pillars of support to maintain obedience … so participation matters. It matters a lot."[22]

What's more, she discovered that there were many more barriers to participation in a violent insurgency as compared to a nonviolent campaign. Primarily because most people aren't willing or able to quit their jobs, use a deadly weapon and become guerilla warriors. Whereas many more people would be willing and able to attend a protest, boycott an industry, wear a t-shirt, hold a sign, march with thousands of other supporters in the streets, and perform many other low-commitment-level acts of civil disobedience that are entirely nonviolent, and less dangerous. In other words, *"in a nonviolent campaign, people can participate when they feel like it; when it counts. But, then they can go home, back to their day job, or their family. They don't have to leave or to underground. They can participate in an ad hoc matter that won't disrupt their daily lives very much."*[23]

Of course, it takes a lot of convincing to get most people to use deadly force against other human beings. Even the U.S. military has to subject new recruits to significant psychological reprogramming in order to mold them into soldiers who are willing to take another human life. Because, with the exception of psychopaths, the average person will not easily pull the trigger on someone arbitrarily, even under combat situations.

In a nonviolent campaign, none of these factors come into play. Participants only need to show up, speak up and behave in ways that come more naturally, such as singing, praying, sitting silently, or shouting. The bar for participation is drastically lower. This makes the success of recruitment and engagement among the populace extremely likely.

Chenoweth also found that nonviolent campaigns were 46% more effective against repressive opponents, compared to only 20% for violent campaigns. In her research, she looked at 3 maximal goals in her data set: Regime change, Enemy occupation and Secession. What she found was that, in 90% of cases, all resistance efforts experienced massive repression from the State level. But, even so, the nonviolent campaigns still outperformed the violent ones by two-to-one. But why?

One reason may be because people seem to be more morally outraged when nonviolent actors are repressed than when violent insurgents are. This means whenever your nonviolent actions are repressed by the State, you're more likely to gain more support for your cause than violent campaigns would receive. Another reason may be because, when you have large numbers of people involved in your campaign, you have a much wider array of available tactics at your disposal. So, instead of either "attack" or "retreat", for example, your nonviolent campaign can employ a variety of methods to maintain pressure on the State, even when you're technically in a passive state or in "retreat" mode. Nonviolent campaigns typically employ two distinct methods of engagement. Those are either concentration—marked by demonstrations, protests, marches, etc.—or dispersion methods— such as boycotts, strikes, economic or social non-participation, etc. By constantly alternating between these two methods, nonviolent campaigns can apply pressure on their oppressors at all times. This sort of relentless tactic is almost impossible to overcome, which is quite often why it nearly always succeeds when utilized deliberately, consistently and nonviolently.

Simply put, nonviolent resistance works so well because it presents fewer obstacles to involvement, attracts greater numbers of participation from the community—at less risk—which, in turn, contributes to enhanced flexibility and innovation. Nonviolence creates a more effective disruption of the status quo and produces the desired results without bloodshed.

NONVIOLENCE CREATES A MORE EFFECTIVE DISRUPTION OF THE STATUS QUO AND PRODUCES THE DESIRED RESULTS WITHOUT BLOODSHED.

In her research, Chenoweth also found that, whenever these coordinated nonviolent efforts were used, they tended to create more long-lasting, peaceful democracies, which were less likely to regress into civil war.[24]

So, does nonviolence work? Yes, clearly it does. We not only have dozens of real-world examples throughout our history where it has worked, we also have excellent research to explain how and why it's a better, and more effective, option than old-fashioned violence. Yet, our addiction to violence remains unchecked. Our devotion to redemptive violence is unwavering. The myth continues to thrive, no matter how many times we debunk it; no matter how many times we prove otherwise.

What can we do to change this? Is there any way to pry these cold, dead lies from the hearts and minds of the collective human consciousness? Can we ever hope to compete with hundreds of years of mythology surrounding the ideal of redemptive violence?

Honestly, I really don't know. But, I'd love to share some stories of what happens when we have the courage to break the narrative and overcome evil with love. That's what we'll talk about next.

CHAPTER 6

LOVING OUR ENEMY

"Only two defining forces have ever offered to die for you: Jesus Christ and The American soldier. One died for your soul. The other died for your freedom."

— UNKNOWN

The air was bitter cold when Julio Diaz stepped off the subway and onto the sidewalk. He had just finished his nightshift and was on his way, as usual, to grab a bite to eat at his favorite diner before heading home to sleep before the sunrise. That's when the young man with the knife approached him.

"Give me your wallet, dude."

Julio froze. He looked at the boy's face under the ballcap. Serious. Frightened. Desperate. He slowly reached back to pull his wallet out of his back pocket. "No trouble, son. No trouble. Here ya go."

As he extended his hand the boy snapped the wallet away like a cobra striking his prey. There was an awkward pause as if neither one of them knew what to do or say next. Julio noticed the boy was shivering.

"Hey, you might need this, too," he said, pulling his jacket off his shoulders. The boy cocked his head sideways in confusion.

"Huh?"

Julio held his jacket out in front of him. "If you're going to be robbing people for the rest of the night, you might as well take my coat. To keep you warm."

The boy blinked at him. "Why are you doing this?"

Julio smiled at him. "Well, if you're willing to risk your freedom for a few dollars, then I guess you must really need the money. I mean, all I wanted to do was get dinner and if you really want to join me … hey, you're more than welcome."

The boy dropped the knife into his back pocket and took the coat, slipping his arms inside. The warmth wrapped around him like an unexpected embrace.

Julio started walking and the boy fell in behind him. They walked in silence the next two blocks until they reached the diner. Julio held the door open for him and they both stepped inside.

Grabbing a booth near the back, they waited for the waitress to drop off the menus. Soon, the manager, the dishwasher and a few of the other customers dropped by to say hello.

"Do you own this place?" the boy asked.

"No, why do you ask that?"

"Because everyone here knows you."

Julio laughed. "No, I just eat here a lot."

"But, you're even nice to the dishwashers," he replied.

"Well, haven't you been taught to be nice to everybody?"

The boy smirked. "Yeah, but I never thought people really did that."

After their orders arrived, Julio started making small talk. "What do you want out of life? What are your dreams?"

The boy paused over his plate of eggs. When he looked up again his face had a deep sadness to it. "I don't know … "

Eventually, the bill arrived. Julio instinctively grabbed it and then said, "Look, I was going to buy you a meal, but I guess this one's on you," he said. "I mean, you've got my wallet. Otherwise, I can't pay for this, ya know?"

The boy sat back.

"Tell ya what," Julio said, "If you give me my wallet back I'll gladly treat you."

Without missing a beat, the boy handed him his wallet. Julio pulled out a few bills and laid them on top of the check, then he pulled out a twenty and pushed it back across the table. "In case you get hungry later."

The boy slowly took the money and slid it into his front pocket. They sat there for a moment looking nervously across the table at one another. That's when Julio asked him for a favor.

"Can I ask you something?"

"What's that?", the boy said.

"Would you give me that knife?"

Without hesitating the boy reached down, pulled out the blade and slid it across the table to Julio.

"Thanks," he said.

"Thank you," the boy said, with tears starting to form in his eyes. "I guess I should go home now."

They walked outside together, shook hands and said goodnight.[25]

Stories like this one may be rare to our ears, but they are true stories. Moments where someone responds to threats of violence with compassion often provide us with examples of what could happen if we tried to love our enemies and bless those who curse us in our everyday lives.

DISARMING HOSPITALITY

On a warm summer night in Washington, DC, a group of eight friends were celebrating an evening together with great food, good wine and laughter at a backyard dinner party. There was much to celebrate. One friend had just opened a new restaurant that week. Others were just glad to be together to spend time with their friends and share delicious food and expensive wine with one another.

Around 10 p.m. the stranger stepped into their yard holding a gun. He held it to the head of one of the women and said, "Give me your money or I'm going to start shooting."

Everyone got silent. They believed him. He kept repeating that mantra: "Give me your money or I'm going to start shooting."

The problem was, no one had any cash on them. They showed him their wallets and their purses. No cash. What now?

At first, they tried talking him down. Guilt came first. "What would your mother say if she could see you now?" one person asked. "I don't have any f---ing mother!" he said. They could feel the tension rising. How long before he started to shoot?

Suddenly one of the women broke the awkward silence. "We're just here celebrating together. Why don't you join us? Have a glass of wine," she said. Her trembling hands held out a full glass of wine to him.

There was a noticeable switch in the atmosphere. Everyone could feel the pressure drop. The man accepted the glass from the woman and took a sip. "Damn, that's a very good glass of wine," he said.

"Have some more," they said, pouring more into his glass. "We have some cheese here, too." The man sat down at their table. He put the gun in his pocket and picked up some cheese.

Silently, the man ate some of the cheese, drank some more of the wine, and then said, almost to himself, "I think I've come to the wrong place."

Everyone sat there together for a moment. The night was surreal. Crickets chirped in the distance. Stars twinkled above them. A light breeze blew the leaves in the trees overhead. "Hey," one of them said. "It's okay." Another added, "We understand. These things happen."

Then, the strangest thing happened. The man looked up at them and asked, "Can I get a hug?"

> ONE-BY-ONE THEY ALL SURROUNDED THE MAN AND WRAPPED THEIR ARMS AROUND HIM IN A COMFORTING EMBRACE. ETERNITY SEEMED FROZEN IN THAT MOMENT.

So, one woman hugged him, then another. Then the man said, "Can we get a group hug?"

One-by-one they all surrounded the man and wrapped their arms around him in a comforting embrace. Eternity seemed frozen in that moment.

Then, as they stepped back, the man said, "I'm sorry." He took his glass of wine and left the party the way he had come.[26]

RADICAL FORGIVENESS

On October 2, 2006, Charles Carl Roberts IV entered the West Nickel Mines School house holding a loaded gun. He proceeded to shoot ten girls, between the ages of 6 and 13 years old, and killed five of them. Then, he turned the gun on himself and took his own life.

While stories like this are all-too-common in our nation today, the reaction of the community was anything but.

This shooting had taken place in the Amish country of Bart Township in Lancaster County, Pennsylvania. The families who lost their daughters were filled with grief over the loss of their children, but they were also filled with something even stronger—the love of Christ.

This is why, instead of responding out of their despair, they followed the Prince of Peace and found the faith to act out the loving example of Jesus.

Just one week after the shooting, the same families who lost their daughters in this senseless and selfish act visited Marie Roberts, the wife of the man who had pulled the trigger and taken his own life.

They boldly, and sincerely, offered their complete forgiveness to her. They invited her to attend the funeral services for their slain daughters. They shared all relief funds sent to them with Mrs. Roberts and her own children who had lost their father that same day. They even attended the funeral of Charles Roberts and offered their loving support to his widow and his children.

THIS REMARKABLE FORGIVENESS. THIS AUDACIOUS KINDNESS. THIS UNCOMMON COMPASSION. IS THERE ANYTHING MORE BEAUTIFUL? OR MORE INSPIRING?

Those people also went to the home of the shooter's mother on the same night as the shooting—not to accuse her of being a bad mother, or to throw rocks through her window—but to wrap her in their arms, weep with her and invite her to stay in their community.

Today, the mother of that shooter works to care for the most seriously injured survivor of this shooting—a young girl—as a way of expressing her gratitude for the love and mercy offered to her and her family on that fateful day.[27]

Is there any other way to describe these reactions to suffering, and violence, and danger than "Christlike"?

This remarkable forgiveness. This audacious kindness. This uncommon compassion. Is there anything more beautiful? Or more inspiring?

We saw this same pattern of radical love and forgiveness in Charleston, South Carolina after nine African Americans were shot during a Bible study at the Emanuel African Methodist Episcopal Church on June 17, 2015.

While some prominent Christian leaders used this tragedy as an opportunity to call for armed security to protect their flock, the true Christlike reactions came from those who had suffered the greatest loss; the bereaved families themselves.

When the killer had been captured, the families of those who had been murdered were allowed to speak to the shooter. One-by-one they each stepped forward to extend forgiveness to the young man who had pulled the trigger and stolen away their mothers, fathers, brothers and sisters.

"No matter how much hate there is in the world, it's no match for love," said Chris Singleton, son of slain Sharonda Singleton. "Love is always stronger than hate."

The daughter of Ethel Lance, addressing the killer directly in court, said, "I will never talk to her ever again. I will never be able to hold her ever again. But I forgive you."

Anthony Thompson, husband of the slain Myra Thompson, echoed Lance's daughter's words. "I forgive you. My family forgives you," he said.

Felecia Sanders, the grandmother who shielded her 5-year-old granddaughter from the gunfire, but lost her son in process, told the killer that the parishioners "welcomed you Wednesday night at our Bible study with open arms." She continued, fighting tears: "You have killed some of the most beautiful people that I know … And it will never be the same. But as we said in Bible study, we enjoyed you. May God have mercy on you."[28]

Alana Simmons, granddaughter of victim Daniel Simmons, said: "Although my grandfather and the other victims died at the hands of hate … everyone's plea for your soul is proof that they lived and loved and their legacies will live on. Hate won't win."

Another relative added, "I am a work in progress and I acknowledge that I am very angry. But we are the family that love built. We have no room for hate. So, we forgive."

WE ARE CALLED TO LOVE EXTRAVAGANTLY AND TO FORGIVE INEXPLICABLY, AND TO DEMONSTRATE TO THE WORLD THAT JESUS IS ALIVE INSIDE OF US.

Where do we find that kind of love? Where does it come from? Are these people just being religious? Are they pretending to love the one who killed their father, or mother, or sister or brother? Or is it possible that the sort of love that Jesus describes in the Sermon on the Mount is actually real?

Out of hate, love can conquer. Out of despair, hope can rise. Out of tragedy, forgiveness can overcome and transcend human emotion. Jesus empowers those who follow Him and put His words into practice. He fills us with real life, and real love that most people can only dream about.

In times of great darkness and despair, this love shines like the sun and puts Jesus on display for everyone to see.

This is why we're called to love our enemies. This is why we are expected to overcome evil with good. Not so we can be door mats, but so that we can demonstrate to the world that the Gospel is real and that His love transforms us into people who can love in the face of tragedy and forgive even the greatest evils.

The message of the Gospel is subversive. It goes against the grain. It makes a real, dramatic, powerful difference at just the right time, and when no one could possibly even expect it.

This is what we are called to, as followers of Christ. We are called to love extravagantly and to forgive inexplicably, and to demonstrate to the world that Jesus is alive inside of us.

UNCOMMON LOVE

There was a time when such reactions weren't so uncommon. In fact, from the very beginning of our faith, it was normative for Christians to endure violence, torture, crucifixion and death at the hands of evil forces. For almost 400 years, this sort of enemy love and radical forgiveness was simply called "Christianity" among the pagans. Not only are there no voices expressing anything other than love for their oppressors for those first three centuries, there are also no examples of any Christian retaliations to defend the innocent or fight back. Instead, we have story after story of martyrs who willingly gave up their lives to share in the sufferings of Christ.

In contrast, if those early Christians had been anything like well-armed American Christians of today, they would no doubt have killed Saul of Tarsus when he came knocking on their doors to carry them away for trial and crucifixion; forever eradicating any opportunity for him to encounter Christ for himself and become the most prolific author of our New Testament scriptures.

FIGHT LIKE CHRIST

As we've said, following Jesus into nonviolent enemy-love does not entail "doing nothing." On the contrary, if one embarks on this path of peace and begins walking in the footsteps of Christ, the one thing you cannot ever do is "nothing" when faced with injustice, or evil, or oppression.

Yes, there is plenty worth fighting for, but for those who pledge their

YES, THERE IS PLENTY WORTH FIGHTING FOR, BUT FOR THOSE WHO PLEDGE THEIR ALLEGIANCE TO THE PRINCE OF PEACE, THERE IS NOTHING WORTH KILLING FOR.

allegiance to the Prince of Peace, there is nothing worth killing for.

We fight, we resist, we react, we overcome and we subvert the violence, or we endure it, or die from it, but we never employ it against another person.

We recognize that everyone is made in the image of God; that everyone is a child of God and dearly loved by God. So, we do everything within our power to introduce love to those who only know hate; to shed light to those who can only see the darkness; to offer mercy to those who have only known pain.

When we share wine with those who threaten us, or we offer hugs instead of hate, when we share our jacket with the mugger, or forgive those who have taken away our dearest friends and family, this is when the Kingdom of God breaks through. This is when darkness is overcome by the light. This is when hate is overwhelmed by forgiveness. This is when love casts out fear.

But, what if we respond in this way and our attacker isn't transformed? What if we try to love our enemies and they remain the same? What if we turn the other cheek and end up losing our lives? What then?

For many of us, the idea of loving in such a radical way only makes sense if it works. But, what if it doesn't work? What then?

Well, to be honest, we could respond to hate with love and end up dead. That is entirely possible. In these examples above, love often worked to disarm the thief and kindness worked to transform the attacker. But, let's get real. Loving our enemies doesn't always work. It didn't work for Jesus. He loved and he still ended up nailed to a cross. It didn't work for Gandhi. He still ended up shot by someone who hated him. It didn't work for Martin Luther King, Jr.. He was assassinated by the sort of person he wanted to change.

So, we must decide up front one thing: Following Jesus into nonviolent enemy-love is something we do because we believe in Christ, not something we do because it always ends with "happily ever after." In fact, whether it works or not, we remain committed to the teachings of Christ. Why? Because this is the sort of person we want to become: someone who loves; someone who forgives; someone who looks like Jesus.

Perhaps this is why Jesus urges his followers to do this one thing before they ever embark on their journey as disciples: "Take up your cross daily." In other words, get it through your head that you are going to die no matter what. Your death is inevitable. Everyone is going to die. Saving your life is not the goal. In fact, if you want to save your life, Jesus says, you will lose it. But, if you lose your life for his sake, you will find it. (See Matthew 16:25)

It comes down to this: If you're going to die anyway, what sort of life do you want to live? Do you want to live a life of love, or a life of violence? Do you want your life to be marked by compassion, forgiveness, mercy, grace and kindness? Or do you want your life to look just like everyone else around you? As Jesus asks us to consider:

> "If you love those who love you in return, what good is that? Doesn't everyone do this? But if you want to become someone who loves like God loves, then love your enemies; bless those who curse you, do good to those who hate you, and then you will become like your Father in Heaven whose love extends even to those who hate and reject Him." (Luke 6:32-33)

Modern Christianity has become so far removed from the way of Christ that we do not live differently, or love differently, than anyone else. In other words, Christ has made no difference whatsoever in our lives.

This is not about being saved. It's not about going to heaven after we die. It's very simply about whether or not we have heard the words of Jesus and decided to put them into practice. Remember, Jesus told us quite explicitly that it's not enough for us to merely know something or believe something. What matters is whether or not we have taken what we know and put it into action.

Unfortunately, many of us have gotten the idea that the blessings come when we know something. We take notes. We study. We highlight. We underline. We may even turn around and teach what we've learned to someone else just to prove we really understand it. But, none of that matters, according to Jesus. To receive the blessing we have to do what he says. There's no other way.

Earlier, we spoke about this Prince of Peace that Isaiah said would come and teach us to walk in the path of peace. We noted that it was only when those people who encountered this Messiah decided to walk in this path that the decision to study war no more and to convert their weapons into garden tools started to happen. This is still the case. Until we decide to walk this path of peace; until we decide to study war no more; until we make up our minds to put these teachings into actual practice, the world will remain unchanged; and we will too.

In other words, the world will change when we change. Jesus came to inspire this transformation within our hearts. He gave us a new way to be human. He showed us a more excellent way: the way of love. Now, the only thing that is left to complete the final step in the process is for us to start living in this new way; walking in this new path; loving in this new and more beautiful way that disarms our enemies, renews our minds, and transforms our world.

But, how do we do this? Immediately so many "what ifs?" and "What abouts?" flood our mind. We imagine all sorts of scenarios where this path of enemy love and nonviolent action seems to run us off the road and over the cliff into the bottomless pit of darkness below. What good can come of this? Aren't we supposed to protect the innocent? Aren't we doing evil if we allow evil to flourish?

Perhaps this is what we should take some time to examine in our next chapter.

CHAPTER 7

EVALUATING IMAGINARY THREATS

"Non-violence honors the humanity of the oppressor, demonstrates belief that God can transform them, and treats the oppressor with dignity and respect. Imagine a world where creative non-violence is the norm rather than exception. That world is worth my life ... and yours."

— J. SWIGART

There were 363 mass shootings in the United States in the first six months of 2021. Keep in mind, a "mass shooting" is defined as an incident where at least four people—other than the shooter—are either wounded or killed by a gunman. During that same time-frame, there were exactly 24,049 gun-related deaths, including 1,166 verified unintentional shootings.[29]

The previous year was called "the deadliest year of gun violence in at least two decades"[30] Possibly because gun ownership in America increased from 32% to 39% in 2020 alone. Simply put, people are afraid. They're worried about the Pandemic creating food shortages, and White Nationalists storming the Capitol, and violent criminals crossing our Southern borders to steal our jobs, and our freedoms and break into our homes, and a few dozen other unrealistic and improbable horrors.[31]

Our media seems almost exclusively focused on creating as much fear as possible. If it's not the 24-hour cable news networks churning out segment-after-segment on why you should fear immigrants, and democrats (or republicans), and deadly viruses, and losing your job, and being evicted, and alien invasions, and serial killers, and murder hornets, and global warming, and … well, you get the picture. It's an endless barrage of all the reasons you should be afraid—all of the time.

One thing we learn in the New Testament is the idea that "perfect love casts out fear" (1 John 4:18), but the opposite is also true: *Perfect fear casts our love.* So, perhaps our minds are being so inundated with this non-stop message of fear that our hearts have no possible chance of being transformed by love.

Our world looks so dangerous. Our nation is under constant threat from enemies within and without. Our way of life is constantly in danger of being eradicated in the blink of an eye. We feel hopeless, helpless and most of all, we feel anything but love for "those people" who are coming after us.

This is the world where Jesus's commands to love our enemies, do good to those who hate us, pray for those who mistreat us, and turn the other cheek to those who strike us seems not only impossible, but completely and totally absurd.

Is Jesus calling us to be the world's punching bag? How does this bring glory to God? How can this possibly accomplish anything good for anyone?

Well, before we jump into that, let's first of all address some of these fears that seem to have hijacked our way of thinking. I mean, we're all afraid that the sky is falling and the world is getting progressively more evil. Most of us would probably argue that the crime rates are worse than ever and that things used to be so much better back when we were younger. But, is that true? Are things really getting worse? Actually, no. Truth be told, things are actually getting progressively better in almost every way. For example, back in the 1800s, more than 40% of America's newborns died before the age of five. Out of the five million immigrants to the United States during that time, roughly 20% of them were slaves. The age of sexual consent in many states was as young as ten years old.[32] What's worse, abortion was not only legal, more than a fifth of all pregnancies during this time ended in abortion[33], and both prostitution and alcoholism were much more common, compared to today.[34] Not to mention, women and black people couldn't vote, native Americans were slaughtered by the millions, husbands could legally abuse their wives, (as long as they didn't kill them, of course), and many of the luxuries and freedoms we enjoy today were nothing more than pipe dreams.

So, yes, things today are much better. Crime rates overall have actually been dropping steadily since the 1990s. In fact, today's national crime rate is half of what it was in 1991, with violent crime dropping 51% and property crime down 43%.[35] Abortion rates have fallen too. There were nearly 200,000 fewer abortions performed in 2017 as compared to 2011, which is a drop to just 13.5%—the lowest rate since abortion became legal nationwide in 1973.[36]

Yes, as we said at the top of this chapter, mass shootings are on the rise over the last few years. But, keep in mind, that many of these shootings are driven by the fear, anxiety and tribalism generated by our media, and by political leaders who demonize the "others" as a way of gaining power and influence. Without this toxic atmosphere of fear, things would most likely be moving in a positive direction. If anything, those who tell us that things are getting worse—when they're actually getting better—are in essence fulfilling their own prophecies by creating enough fear to generate an increase in mass shootings.

So, of course, we have plenty of problems to overcome, but most of what drives our fear—violent crime, declining morality, loss of personal freedoms, etc.—are, statistically, on the upward path towards improvement. So, why aren't we hearing about it? Well, it turns out that fear sells.

Author David Altheide has spent many years documenting how the media uses the language of fear to keep people in a constant state of uncertainty and endless unease. As he notes, this pervasive aura of fear ends up changing us from the inside out in ways most of us cannot detect:

> "Social life starts to change because of it, and we start altering our lives ... We don't go out as much. Architecturally, we protect ourselves with gated communities, high walls and no windows. Public space begins to decline."[37]

Over time we are programmed to feel afraid for our safety, we begin to believe that the world is more violent, when crime is actually in decline. We become convinced that threats to our health and safety and way of life are everywhere and all we can do is lock our doors and stay away from "those people" out there who only want to hurt us, or rob us, or perhaps even kill us if they had the chance.[38]

Dr. Deborah Serani, a psychiatrist writing for Psychology Today Magazine noted:

> "In previous decades, the journalistic mission was to report the news as it actually happened, with fairness, balance, and integrity. However, capitalistic motives associated with journalism have forced much of today's television news to look to the spectacular, the stirring, and the controversial as news stories. It's no longer a race to break the story first or get the facts right. Instead, it's to acquire good ratings in order to get advertisers, so that profits soar ... "[39]

She goes on to explain:

"Fear-based news programming has two aims. The first is to grab the viewer's attention ... The second aim is to persuade the viewer that the solution for reducing the identified fear will be in the news story ... What occurs psychologically for the viewer is a fragmented sense of knowing what's real, which sets off feelings of hopelessness and helplessness - experiences known to worsen depression."[40]

When people are afraid, they are easy to manipulate. They are quick to adopt an "Us vs Them" posture and will more readily participate in scapegoating where an entire people group - political party, religious group, race, or other faction - may be pinned with the blame for whatever threat has been identified, whether real or imagined.

In his book, *In the Name of Identity: Violence and the Need to Belong*, author Amin Maalouf accurately identifies tribalism and fear as catalysts for violence and genocide. Throughout history we can recognize the way those in power have rallied people together under an identity rooted in nationalism and leveraged that to incite large-scale acts of violence and war—all in the name of identity: one tribe against the other; one religion against another; one nation against the other.[41]

So, we can see that almost everything our media has conditioned us to fear isn't actually something we need to worry about. We can also see how fear has been used to manipulate us and control us. As Franklin D. Roosevelt said in 1933, *"We have nothing to fear but fear itself."*

What's more, we have numerous examples in Scripture where we are compelled to embrace love and refuse fear-based thinking. For example, every time God appears to someone, or sends an angel or messenger to speak to them, the very first phrases spoken are either *"Fear not!"* or *"Do not be afraid!"*, and of course we cannot forget this important reminder:

> "For God has not given us a spirit of fear, but of power and of love and of a sound mind." (2 Tim. 1:7)

Simply put, if we allow ourselves to be ruled by fear, and swayed by all the voices of fear in our media, we will become paralyzed and completely unable to do the very thing we were created to do: Love!

So, let's get back to our questions at the top of this chapter about whether or not Jesus is calling us to be doormats, and what possible good could come from our suffering at the hands of violent men.

NO DOORMATS

At first blush, Jesus's commands can really seem as if the goal is for us to just line up for our butt-kicking with a hearty shout of, "Thank you, sir! May I have another?" But that's not the point. At all.

So, if Jesus isn't looking to create an army of wimps and losers, what is the goal here? Why are we instructed not to respond to violence with more violence? What is the point of this sort of teaching? Let's return to the passage in Matthew again:

> "You have heard that it was said, 'Eye for eye, and tooth for tooth.' *But I tell you, do not resist an evil person. If anyone slaps you on the right cheek, turn to them the other cheek also.* And if anyone wants to sue you and take your shirt, hand over your coat as well. If anyone forces you to go one mile, go with them two miles. Give to the one who asks you, and do not turn away from the one who wants to borrow from you.
>
> *"You have heard that it was said, 'Love your neighbor and hate your enemy.' But I tell you, love your enemies and pray for those who*

persecute you, that you may be children of your Father in heaven.
He causes his sun to rise on the evil and the good, and sends rain
on the righteous and the unrighteous. *If you love those who love
you, what reward will you get? Are not even the tax collectors doing
that? And if you greet only your own people, what are you doing
more than others? Do not even pagans do that? Be Holy, therefore,
as your heavenly Father is Holy."* (Matt. 5:38-48, emphasis mine)

The short answer to "What is Jesus up to here?" is simply
this: Humanity has been caught in this "tit-for-tat", back-and-
forth, "You hurt me so I'll hurt you" sort of escalating behavior
from day one. We harm others because they harm us. We end-
lessly retaliate against the violent with more violence until small
disagreements grow into large ones, which grow into fights, and
then into wars, and eventually into genocides. Once the cycle
begins, it's almost impossible for us to break out of this way
of thinking, and behaving. We also know that, at this time in
history, the Jewish people were under the oppressive rule of the
Roman empire. Many were desperately seeking a Messiah who
would lead an armed insurrection against their captors and liber-
ate the people to restore the nation of Israel to power once again.
This, specifically, was what Jesus was wanting them to abandon.
Why? Because he knew that if they did not take a sudden detour
from this path, it would inevitably lead them to complete and
utter annihilation: the destruction of their Temple, the end of
their priesthood and the cessation of their daily sacrifices, and
millions dead. In essence, the end of the age.

So, when Jesus urges them to consider an alternate path, it's
about helping them avoid this grim outcome. He knows that,
unless they abandon this course of action, they will be destroyed.
He wants them to understand this very simple principle: "If you
want to experience something you've never experienced before,
you'll have to do something you've never done before." Or, to put

it another way, "The system you have now is perfectly designed to create the results you are now experiencing." Do you hate the way the Romans keep oppressing you? Maybe try doing something different next time. In fact, try doing something almost no one has ever done before. When they strike you, turn the other cheek. When they force you to walk a mile, walk two miles. Not only will your unexpected responses surprise them, it just might disarm them and draw them into a more introspective analysis of the injustice they are perpetrating. Even if not, at least you will be doing exactly what your Heavenly Father does when the pagans offend Him—love them anyway!

THE SYSTEM YOU HAVE NOW IS PERFECTLY DESIGNED TO CREATE THE RESULTS YOU ARE NOW EXPERIENCING. In another sense, whenever we respond to those who seek to harm us with such surprising acts of kindness, it allows the Kingdom of God to break in. Suddenly, those who have never known mercy are surrounded by it; those who have never experienced love are engulfed in it; those who have only heard the faintest whispers of grace find themselves powerless to speak as it washes over them.

This is why Jesus wants us to respond to evil and violence with love. Because those who have known love the least are the very people who need love the most. How else will this great and wondrous love of God that dwells within us ever reach those people?

The moments where we experience direct expressions of hatred are exactly the moments when the true power of love can really shine. For those who have eyes to see, these are opportunities for the light to push back darkness.

I believe this is what the Apostle Paul is referring to when he says:

> Do not take revenge, my dear friends, but leave room for God's wrath, for it is written: "It is mine to avenge; I will repay," says

the Lord. On the contrary: 'If your enemy is hungry, feed him; if he is thirsty, give him something to drink. In doing this, you will heap burning coals on his head.' Do not be overcome by evil, but overcome evil with good." (Romans 12:19-21)

Sadly, many Christians take this to mean: *"God is going to make them pay in the Afterlife. Just be nice to them now because one day they will meet God and get what's coming to them."* They even think that the phrase *"in doing this you will heap burning coals on his head"* is about making those people suffer shame, or frustration. But that's not at all what Paul's talking about.

The point here is this: If God is the One who will settle accounts one day, then, for now, feed your enemy and make sure they have something to drink if they're thirsty. This is how you will satisfy your inner desires to repay their evil with more evil—which is not Christlike!

On the contrary, here's how to overcome evil—by doing good to those who harm you. Isn't this the way God overcomes evil? Didn't Jesus overcome evil by forgiving those who crucified him, and laying down his life for those he loved, and even those who didn't love him? That's your example! Do what God does; show mercy to the unmerciful and love to the unlovely.

> DIDN'T JESUS OVERCOME EVIL BY FORGIVING THOSE WHO CRUCIFIED HIM, AND LAYING DOWN HIS LIFE FOR THOSE HE LOVED, AND EVEN THOSE WHO DIDN'T LOVE HIM? THAT'S YOUR EXAMPLE!

As Jesus has already told us: This is how God treats His enemies, and that's why you should, too. So, the way God will "avenge," or "repay" those who mistreat you is exactly consistent with the way we are commanded to respond: with love, not vengeance. So, God's wrath, in this passage, is revealed to be an overwhelming and irresistible wave of kindness and mercy. Those coals of fire are not intended to burn, or torture, or destroy anyone; they're designed to purify and restore everyone "so that we may share in the Holiness of God" (Hebrews 12:5-11)

Jesus doesn't want us to become doormats. He wants us to become living examples of his love, mercy and kindness. So that those who have never known those realities can experience them for the very first time, and in the most unexpected ways.

JESUS DOESN'T WANT US TO BECOME DOORMATS. HE WANTS US TO BECOME LIVING EXAMPLES OF HIS LOVE, MERCY AND KINDNESS.

Our mission—and our heart's desire—is to love those who have never really experienced it, to forgive those who don't believe they deserve it, and to show mercy to those who have never truly known it before.

WHAT GOOD WILL COME FROM DYING?

Quite often, as I'm discussing these sorts of ideas with people, I'll hear the question: "What possible good could come from allowing your enemies to kill you?" or "What good can you do for the Kingdom—or your family—if you're dead?"

On one level, these questions make sense. The point can't possibly be that our goal is to end up dead, right? What would that accomplish?

Well, let's keep in mind that Jesus didn't consider dying in the act of loving his enemies to be a failure or a waste of time. On the contrary, it does almost seem to be the entire point. Here's what I mean: If we cannot see the value of following Jesus to the point of death, we've missed the whole thing. Jesus was quite clear that following him and walking his path would involve dying to self—and yes, our actual death, not some metaphorical sense of dying to this value system or that way of thinking, but honest-to-goodness death with a capital "D."

This is why Jesus tells us that, before we can ever become one of his followers, we have to take up our cross daily, die to ourselves—yes spiritually but quite possibly physically as well—and put his words into practice. (See Luke 9:23; 14:27, Matt. 10:38; 16:24, and Mark 8:34)

Maybe we've spiritualized these verses so much that we've convinced ourselves that Jesus is only talking about death and dying as metaphors rather than as actual death and dying. But, a quick survey of the rest of the New Testament, and the first 300 years of Church History, reveals the sobering truth—millions of people who put Jesus's words into practice ended up very, very dead.

For most of us, today, Christianity has been repackaged into an accessory that complements the upholstery of the vehicle you're driving as you engage in the highspeed pursuit of life, liberty and happiness. We no longer see the act of following Jesus the way those early disciples saw it: as the end of your life and the beginning of something radically different.

Our goal as followers of Jesus is not to win every argument, survive every encounter, and overcome every obstacle until we burst into Heaven one day to the sound of thunderous applause. On the contrary, our goal is to look like Jesus. That means sometimes we stand up for injustice and we go down. Sometimes we speak for the oppressed and we get arrested. Sometimes we turn the other cheek and we get crucified. But, in those moments, we look for our opportunity to look someone in the eye and say, "I forgive you and I love you," just before we breathe our last.

Everyone dies. So, our death should come as no surprise to us. The opportunity Jesus provides us with is to let our life, and our death, reflect the love of Christ to the world around us. If we're going to live, let us live for Christ. If we're going to die, let us share in the sufferings of Christ and use it as an opportunity to reflect the beauty of His great love to as many people as we can.

ALTERNATIVE SOLUTIONS

So, if you're suddenly faced with a situation where an intruder has entered your home and is holding a gun or a knife to your spouse's head, what should you do? Some would want us to believe that our only options are to either do absolutely nothing, or to pull out our guns and blow the person's head off. But, are those really the only options? Of course not. You could make them a sandwich, or sing them a song, or offer to pray for them, or give them a hug, or fall on your knees to pray, or literally dozens of other things rather than take their life. In fact, there are several real-life situations where an armed intruder was thwarted by nearly all of those suggested actions above. Violence is not the only option, nor is it the best option if your desire is to obey Christ and to allow the love of God to break into a desperate situation.

But, what if you try those things and it doesn't work? What if the gunman ends up killing you in the process? What then? What possible good could come from this scenario? Well, I love the way my friend Benjamin L. Corey answers this one:

> "Let's say an intruder broke into my house to steal my television or raid my medicine cabinet. I accidentally walk in on what's happening and end up getting attacked. Instead of reaching for something that could be used as a weapon, I pass on all opportunities to kill my "enemy" … let's also say that passing on those opportunities costs me my very life—I die, and they live.

> "Here's two things that could potentially happen that would play right into my master plan to keep inviting more and more people into this Jesus thing:

"One: The person who killed me, while sitting in their jail cell, is going to have a lot of time to think about it. In doing so, my hope would be that they'd start asking some questions about why I didn't try to kill them when I had the chance. As they dug into my story, they'd find out the reason why I didn't try to kill them was because I believed with all of my being that they had infinite worth and value to God– and that they were worth dying for. They would then potentially see that I was filled with a radical, self sacrificial love for them which I hope would spark a new question: "why the hell did that guy believe that about me?" This question would lead them to only one answer: Jesus.

" … By trading my life for theirs, an enemy could potentially spend the rest of their natural life asking the question, "why did he love me so much?" and every time, the *only* answer it would lead to would be, Jesus. If I am thinking "long-game" for the Kingdom of God, that's the right answer even if it seems like sheer foolishness in the eyes of the world. However, Jesus taught that whoever loses his life for the sake of the Kingdom will find it again [and that the opposite is true too]—and call me crazy, but I believe him.

"Two: The second potential impact would be the exponential discussion about Jesus that could potentially happen far and wide. It's not often that someone willingly gives their life in place of an enemy's life—and when they do, it generates some buzz … If I were to give my own life in order to allow my enemy to live, people would talk about it because that's a pretty crazy thing to do. But when they did, they'd be forced to talk about this Jesus guy who I've given my life to. That could be potentially huge for the Kingdom– perhaps even bigger than anything I could accomplish while still living.

"Is it true that dying for an enemy is a poor use of your life? Not at all! In fact, if our dedication is to building the Kingdom and making it as big and as crowded as we possibly can– over and above temporal self-preservation– giving our lives for our enemies might actually be one of the most practical and valuable things we could do."[42]

Maybe what's missing most for us is simply a shifting of our perspective about our lives here and now. What is our purpose? What would make our lives meaningful? How could following Jesus all the way to the grave be a bad thing? What better way to demonstrate the life-changing love of Christ to those who have never experienced it than to love everyone—even our oppressors—until it either changes them, or kills us, or both? If we're going to die, why not let it mean something? If we're going to live, why not try to walk as much in the loving character of Christ as possible?

INTERLUDE

In your mind's eye, you see Jesus walking the path of peace.
He reaches a bend in the road ahead and turns to see if you're coming.

You hesitate.

"Will it work?"

It works if you walk it, comes the reply.

"But what if I die?", you wonder.

You were dying anyway.

"Are you trying to kill me? Is that what this is about?"

Your death is inevitable. But shouldn't your life mean something?

You wait. You calculate. You ponder.

"What about these situations I may encounter along the way where violence is my only alternative?"

Are you asking for permission to leave the path? We've barely even started the journey.

You look down and see the path begins just ahead of you. Your feet still lingering on the grass that grows thick around the threshold.

Love is never easy. We have to count the cost.

This is the meaning of life; to live it.

This is the purpose of love, to receive it and then to give it back.

Like breathing in, and breathing out.

You can do it. You're already doing it now.

"But, if I give without asking anything in return ... if I love so selflessly, what's in it for me?"

Love is its own reward. Love is better than life.

"But, what will become of me if I risk everything this way?"

You will become like me.

You step back and ask, "Crucified? Tortured?"

There comes a sigh, and then the word,

Resurrected.

You pause. As if contemplating a sermon.

If only you could write something down and fold it and place it inside of a book for later.

How much time has passed? How long have you lingered on this journey? You look up and see

The Messiah is patiently waiting for you to take your first steps.

You feel old now. The grass around your feet has grown so tall.

Take your time. I know this isn't easy.

Eternity waits.

What you fear is death. What you forfeit is life; the life of Christ.

You feel despair begin to rise within you, cold.

Like a chill that sweeps through your bloodstream.

"They will despise me, reject me,

Humiliate me."

As they did with me.

"They will mock me and hate me … "

As with me?

"I will be alone"

No. I will never leave you, nor forsake you, my child.

Looking down, you see your feet are now on this path.

Fear grips your heart.

My love, let it strengthen you. Fear cannot thrive between us.

"But, what will people say?", you wonder.

"No one walks this path anymore."

Very few. Will you?

Your eyes meet his. Your heart swells.

You feel your feet beginning to move.

CHAPTER 8

THE WAY WE WERE

"If the church were as willing to share its resources and personnel for the mission of Christ as it is to share them with the State in warfare, it would doubtless have had a much greater impact for good in the world than it has"

— MYRON S. AUGSBURGER[43]

Anyone who undertakes the study of the early Church and of Christianity in its infancy during the first 300 years or so, will find themselves marveling at the sheer audacity of those followers who took the teachings of Jesus as their blueprint for daily living. They will see how ordinary it was for followers of Christ to suffer torture and even face death for refusing to declare that Caesar was Lord. "We have no King but Christ!" was their battle cry, and one-by-one, hundreds of thousands of them—perhaps millions—went to their deaths embracing their Lord's commands on loving their enemies and refusing to resist those who wished to do them harm.

The reason why they did this may not be as obvious to us as we presume. It wasn't because they saw this persecution as their opportunity to resist paganism, or to refuse to cooperate with an unchristian Empire. No, it was much more than that. Because today many Christians assume that those early Christian martyrs were dying for their faith because their government was specifically pagan. In other words, we read back into their story our own narrative, and if we do this we will totally miss the point. You see, it's not because Rome was "unchristian" that they followed Christ's commands in this way. What I mean is, if Rome had

MANY CHRISTIANS TODAY ASSUME THAT THOSE EARLY CHRISTIANS ONLY RESISTED THE ROMAN EMPIRE IN THEIR DAY BECAUSE THEIR GOVERNMENT WAS SO EVIL OR "ANTI-CHRISTIAN", BUT ACCORDING TO THOSE EARLY CHRISTIANS THIS IS NOT THE CASE.

been a "Christian" empire, it would still not have been acceptable for those Christians to pledge allegiance to Rome, or to Caesar. As Tertullian phrased it in his Apology:

> "Yes, and the Caesars too would have believed on Christ, if either the Caesars had not been necessary for the world, or if Christians could have been Caesars."[44]

This is a critical point for us to understand. Many Christians today assume that those early Christians only resisted the Roman Empire in their day because their government was so evil or "anti-Christian", but according to those early Christians this is not the case. They understood something that we have not understood: *That Christ's Kingdom is incompatible with any and every other kingdom of this world.*

In other words, to those early Christians, the idea of a "Christian Nation" would be in the same category as a "Square Circle," it would be an oxymoron that, to them, would have been simply absurd.

One of the reasons we have a hard time seeing this incongruity is that we live in a post-Constantinian world where the Church and the State have been wedded together in such a way that we find no trouble with the concept of Christ's Kingdom being aligned with the interests of our nation. We sing hymns in our Churches like "Onward Christian Soldiers" and we proudly display our nation's flag in the sanctuary, or raise it up on a pole outside our churches *above* the Christian flag, and we never think twice about it.

The early Christians would have seen these activities as a direct betrayal of Christ and His Kingdom. But, today, we not only see nothing wrong with this, we become offended if anyone tries to suggest that our nation's flag be removed from the church, or that Christians shouldn't join the military.

This complete shift in perspective within the Church is due to the influence of the Roman Emperor, Constantine the Great on Christianity.

Although Constantine was not even a member of a church, his influence on Christianity today is equal, if not greater than, that of Paul the Apostle and even Jesus Himself.

As the first Christian Emperor of Rome, Constantine declared himself to be a Christian at the age of 40 when he had what he described as a supernatural encounter with Christ at the Battle of Milvian Bridge in 312 A.D. In his vision, the night before the battle, Constantine says that he saw the sign of Christ in the sky—not the cross but the Chi-Rho, which is a symbol marked by the first two letters of Christ's name in Greek—and heard a voice saying, "By this sign you shall conquer." In response, Constantine had this Chi Rho symbol painted on his soldier's shields and the next day they defeated their enemies in battle.

It might be prudent at this point to stop and ask ourselves if Jesus would actually speak to someone and promise them that he would help them kill their enemies in battle or not. Personally, I cannot ever imagine Jesus—the Prince of Peace—who told Pilate, "My Kingdom is not of this world. If it were my disciples would fight," turning around later to tell another Roman ruler,

"Let me help you kill your enemies in battle using my initials as a sign of power." Can you?

Another sign that Constantine's "conversion" story might not be legitimate is when we learn that, after this, he put his own sons to death and killed his wife at the request of his mother. Constantine is also known to have hated the crucifix because it showed Jesus in a posture of weakness. For him, the cross was a sign of power. He seems to have had no understanding of Jesus as a suffering servant, preferring instead to fashion for himself a version of Christ as a triumphant, powerful god who would bless his bloody escapades as a warrior and a conqueror.[45]

What's more, even though Constantine publicly declared himself to be a Christian, we know that he also continued to hold the title of "Pontifex Maximus" which signified his leadership of the pagan priesthood.

Knowing all of this, we have to ask ourselves why the Church allowed a man like this to influence the way they worshipped and practiced their faith? Maybe it was because he was their largest financial supporter? Or because he ended the brutal persecutions of his predecessors? Or because he gave them non-profit, tax-exempt status in the Empire? Perhaps it was because he promoted several of the clergy to high-ranking offices within the Empire? Or because he built large temples for them to worship in?

Whatever the reason, Constantine *was* allowed to dictate to the Church how and when and where they would worship God. Instead of meeting in the home and sharing a meal together, Constantine mandated that Christians meet in the pagan temples which he had provided for them. Instead of a shared and open dialog of faith, Constantine instituted a liturgy which looked very much like that of the pagan's, and of the Roman Empire itself. Worship services were presided over by the clergy who held power much like a king or an emperor. The members of the church were no longer treated as dearly loved members of a family but were treated as peasants to be taxed (via the tithe) and ruled over like subjects.

Of course, the other major shift instituted by Constantine was the merging of the Church and the State. Under his rule, the number of Christians in the Roman military surged. Christians who once refused to pledge allegiance to Rome or to Caesar now took up arms to fight for the Empire and even killed other Christians within one generation after Constantine.

THE OTHER MAJOR SHIFT INSTITUTED BY CONSTANTINE WAS THE MERGING OF THE CHURCH AND THE STATE. UNDER HIS RULE, THE NUMBER OF CHRISTIANS IN THE ROMAN MILITARY SURGED.

As UCLA professor, historian and New Testament scholar, Dr. Scott Bartchy explains, Constantine's influence on the Church was extremely unfortunate:

> "We're still trying to get out from under the cloud that he put over the Church. Basically, Constantine decides in the fourth century that he's going to become the sugar daddy of the Christian faith because there have been four waves of attempts to get rid of the Christians up to his reign, which involved fierce persecutions. So, if you and I were alive at that time we would have all known somebody who had been under persecution by the Empire. Constantine shows up and says he's going to stop all of this and, of course, we have to wonder how else he could have done this without God's Spirit being at work on his heart? Be careful, though. I would caution you not to believe him until he puts his sword away. Personally, I don't think Constantine ever got it. I don't think he ever really understood Jesus."[46]

To Bartchy, one of the most fundamental ironies in the history of culture occurred at the Council of Nicea:

> "This was the first time the leaders of the Christian movement are called together for this big ecumenical meeting. They've been doing fine for hundreds of years without having any such

meeting, but Constantine wants to know who wears the white hats and who wears the black hats," he says. "So, Constantine calls all of these people together and he makes the first speech, stating namely that Jesus is the very same essence and substance of the Father. Nobody had ever talked that way before, but he wants an ideology, he wants unity, he wants to tie the Empire together, which has been divided. He makes sure that Christians are the glue that hold it all together and he wants what they think about God to be united."[47]

One of the things that's largely not known is that Constantine himself was already a Monotheist prior to his conversion to Christianity. As Bartchy says:

"He's not leaving Polytheism to become a Monotheist when he decides to become favorable to the Christians. Before that he worshipped one God whom he was willing to call, along with the other traditional names of the high God, either Zeus among the Greeks, or Jupiter among the Romans. But Zeus and Jupiter are both kick-ass gods. In any case, that's who he worships and so when Constantine stands up and says that Jesus is God he's saying that Jesus is the son of Zeus, a kick-ass god. We still haven't recovered from this. That's why we still have people thinking it's appropriate to kill people in the name of God."[48]

To this day the Christian church continues to meet in the same pagan temple system, with a select clergy held in honor as small kings who rule over the people and maintain the building, and their own livelihood, via the taxing of the peasants through the tithe. They also gladly support the military, send their children off to fight and die for their nation, and fly the flag of their country above their own Christian symbols.

Many who are Christians today aren't even aware of the influence that Constantine had on their faith and continue to read the New Testament as if the references to "Church" and "worship" found there corresponds to the sort of church life they experience. They read passages like Romans 13 as if the Apostle

Paul's point was that Christians should support and even join the government's use of the sword, even though, at the time Paul wrote those words the Church was suffering under the cruel reign of the Emperor Nero who was actively killing Christians and persecuting the Church.

So, if we acknowledge that Constantine's influence over the Church has been devastating, and if we can see that Christians prior to his influence would have never submitted to such notions, what are we to do? How should we respond? Well, my hope is that we would allow Jesus to lead us once again. This would involve a radical shift of our mindset regarding Church and State. It would involve a total rejection of participation in the government, politics, the military and even law enforcement. Not everyone is ready for that kind of shift. Nationalism and political tribalism have become the norm for most Christians today. Breaking free of this won't be easy, but I do believe it's possible.

THE SAVAGE SWORD OF JESUS?

Constantine's perversion of Jesus from the Prince of Peace to the symbol of an Empire's power to rule by the sword is our first detour from the path that leads us to peace, but it's not the last. There have been numerous other attempts to subvert Christ's radical enemy-loving approach into a more flexible version of a Messiah who is pro-war and aligned with the State.

One such attempt was during World War II, under the reign of Hitler. In an interview with Vulture Magazine, writer Grant Morrison talked about how this twisted version of Jesus inspired him to create a comic book called "The Savage Sword of Jesus" based on the Nazi's Positive Christianity project which, " ... recast Christ as a proactive Aryan rather than a meek Jew," says

Morrison. "Obviously, I had done a lot of research … and I came across this interesting idea … [how] the Nazis had attempted to rebrand Christianity, and rebrand Christ, specifically. Take him away from the gentle and peace-loving character of the Gospels, and to transform him into a Nordic and brutish and violent Messiah."[49]

As reported in Vulture magazine:

> "The idea of stories being changed to fit a narrative rings true with Morrison, especially in this current political climate: 'We're living in a time when it's quite clear how even the most pacifist stories or narratives that one time were a lot more positive, can be perverted to stand in as catalysts for violence and mayhem. Especially now that we live in a world where we've seen that lies can easily be overlooked, and where celebrity culture is more powerful than the truth, and where people can quite happily twist any narrative to suit any new narrative, and almost twist narratives into their complete opposites, which is what the Nazis tried to do with the Gospels."[50]

Sound familiar? To me, it sounds frighteningly familiar. Because so many American Christians have pretty much already done this same thing theologically. They've created a version of Jesus that is wrapped in an American flag, who is pro-war, who approves of violence, who condones torture, who supports us when we turn away refugees, and who can't stand to be in the presence of "sinners."

Anyone who reads the actual New Testament scriptures will find that Jesus isn't any of those things. And yet, we seem to have no trouble whatsoever embracing a Jesus we have made in our own Nationalistic, Patriotic, and violent image.

For me, going back to read the words of those pre-Constantinian Church Fathers is like taking a much-needed cold shower that cleanses my soul and awakens me from a long slumber. Suddenly, in their words, I can see a drastic difference between the nonviolent, enemy-loving Christ-followers of the early Church and the sort of compromised Christianity we've developed today where to love Jesus is synonymous with serving in the military, waving your nation's flag and defending your home with deadly force.

Not that Christians should step back from the problems of this world and do nothing, of course. As we've said many times already, to follow the nonviolent, enemy-loving path of Christ is not for the faint of heart. It takes enormous courage to face an armed opponent with nothing in your hands but mercy, knowing full-well that your life may be taken from you in a heartbeat. But, this is why Jesus calls us up-front to count the cost before walking in his path of peace. He urges us to consider our lives already lost for the sake of His Kingdom. Taking up our cross is more than a metaphor for our spiritual death, it's a very real symbol of our actual death in the course of putting his words into daily practice. Giving up our lives for his sake is how we find true life. Our goal is not to try to save our lives, it's to surrender our lives for the sake of loving others—even if it kills us.

> **IT TAKES ENORMOUS COURAGE TO FACE AN ARMED OPPONENT WITH NOTHING IN YOUR HANDS BUT MERCY, KNOWING FULL-WELL THAT YOUR LIFE MAY BE TAKEN FROM YOU IN A HEARTBEAT.**

I love how Myron Augsburger frames this new way of living the Christian life:

> "When troops move to take a beachhead, they do so with the conscious plan that they will sacrifice thousands of men. What if the Christian church moved into the world with the same convictions? What if we had a conscious plan to follow [Jesus] even though it might cost many lives? ... it would appear that before the Christian church justifies giving the lives of so many of its people in military involvement it should look at the greater sin

of being unwilling to sacrifice lives of affluent ease for the cause of building the Kingdom of Christ."[51]

This is what it should mean for us to follow Christ. More than a statement of what we believe, or where we go to Church, or what doctrines we mentally assent to, the very notion of being a "Christian" has always primarily been about putting the teachings and actions of Jesus into daily practice so that those around us look at our lives and see a "little Christ."

Our faith should be about putting what we say we believe into practice. Not merely a club we belong to, or what brand of religion we prefer. In the same way someone is a Jew because they follow the Law of Moses, or someone is a Buddhist because they follow the teachings of Buddha, or someone is a Muslim because they are devoted to the teachings of Mohammed, we as followers of Christ must also be identified as people who live and die by the teachings of Jesus, the Prince of Peace, who came to show us a path that leads us to beat our swords into plowshares and study war no more.

Are we walking on this path? Are we serious about following Jesus in this way? If we're not, that's fine. We should just be honest with ourselves, and with God, about who we're actually following and what pattern we want our lives to reflect.

The exciting thing, to me, is that if those who call ourselves "Christian" really would walk this path laid out for us by Jesus, we could totally end war by the end of this year. I'm serious. How? By simply refusing to fight, laying down our weapons and pledging allegiance to Christ alone. If every Christian did this, the ability of our nation to wage war would evaporate overnight. Because you cannot fight a war without soldiers, and the vast majority of soldiers—at least in the United States Army—are Christians. According to the Department of Defense, recent administrative data focused on active duty personnel shows that, as of January, 2019, approximately 70 percent of soldiers were Christians.[52] That means that if every American Christian in the military would refuse to go to war, our nation's ability to engage in armed conflict would completely vanish.

Now, I know that to some of us that sounds like treason, or a threat to National Security, and guess what? It *is* a threat to National Security! That's why the Romans executed Jesus; because they recognized his teachings of enemy-love and nonviolent resistance were a threat to the Empire. It's exactly why Constantine bamboozled the Christians of his day to stop resisting the power of Rome and become willing participants in the growth and expansion of the Empire; believing that doing so was synonymous with their Christian faith. Because the teachings of Jesus are a serious threat to those who hope to expand their national borders, advance military

> BY PLACING CHRIST ON HIS SHIELD, HE PLACED A SWORD IN THEIR HANDS—AND EVENTUALLY INTO THE HEARTS AND MINDS—OF THOSE VERY SAME CHRISTIANS WHO ONCE VALIANTLY SUFFERED UNDER ROMAN PERSECUTIONS.

might, and dominate surrounding nations by threat of violence, Empires must either eradicate Christ's nonviolent teachings by force, or subvert them under the flag of nationalism, patriotism and militarism. Constantine discovered that violence did nothing but strengthen the Christian resolve to continually resist, and so he brilliantly adopted the tactic known as "if you can't beat'em, join'em", or get them to join you. By placing Christ on his shield, he placed a sword in their hands—and eventually into the hearts and minds—of those very same Christians who once valiantly suffered under Roman persecutions. Now, Christians think nothing of using the sword to defend the Empire, and look suspiciously at anyone who dares to question the use of violence to keep the peace and advance their nation's interests around the globe.

The power to fulfill the prophecy of Isaiah is within our grasp right now—more than at any other time in history, actually. Because there are more Christians alive today than there were 2,000 years ago, and because there are more Christians in the military around the globe than ever before. This means we have the power to end war in our lifetime. But will we?

You might be surprised to learn that Christians have come together to end war throughout history. One of the most amazing examples was during World War I when, about five months into the conflict, in the week leading up to Christmas day, roughly 100,000 French, German and British soldiers simply stopped fighting along the Western Front. They crossed trenches to exchange gifts, mingle, share food, and wish one another a Merry Christmas. They also exchanged prisoners, sang carols, and played a few games of football instead of trying to kill one another. As one British soldier wrote in a letter about the experience:

> "We are having the most extraordinary Christmas Day imaginable. A sort of unarranged and quite unauthorized but perfectly understood and scrupulously observed truce exists between us and our friends in front. The funny thing is it only seems to exist in this part of the battle line—on our right and left we can all hear them firing away as cheerfully as ever. The thing started last night—a bitter cold night, with white frost—soon after dusk when the Germans started shouting 'Merry Christmas, Englishmen' to us. Of course, our fellows shouted back and presently large numbers of both sides had left their trenches, unarmed, and met in the debatable, shot-riddled, no man's land between the lines. Here the agreement—all on their own—came to be made that we should not fire at each other until after midnight tonight. The men were all fraternizing in the middle [we naturally did not allow them too close to our line]

and swapped cigarettes and lies in the utmost good fellowship. Not a shot was fired all night."[53]

As beautiful as this moment was, it was all-too-brief and soldiers were eventually forced by their superiors to return to fighting under threat of court martial. Still, it shows that we can end war and violence if we want to. We could also end World Hunger if we wanted to. But, we don't. Why? Because the conditions that create poverty make so much wealth for so many people that it's nearly impossible to imagine letting go of those things for the sake of others. But perhaps that is a discussion for another time.

Maybe we need to stop and ask ourselves what sort of Christians we want to be. Do we want to look more like those who subvert the peaceful, enemy-loving image of Christ into a savage warrior who slays his enemies? Or do we want to look more like those early Christians who refused to fight and chose to love everyone—even those who persecuted them—out of a sincere devotion to the teachings of Jesus who had shown them a better way to live?

CHAPTER 9

ANSWERING HARD QUESTIONS

"As long as it is assumed that war is always an available option, we will not be forced to imagine any alternative to war."

— STANLEY HAUERWAS

What if my son, daughter, brother, sister, father, mother, best friend, etc. is or was in the military or a veteran? Do they have blood on their hands? Are they forgiven? What should I do?
Before I get into this one, I must once again stress that the purpose of this book is not to point fingers at those who have sincerely loved Christ and found themselves serving in the military or in law enforcement. The early Christians certainly had very strong convictions against these things, primarily because it involved swearing an allegiance to the State, and participation in the kingdoms which rival the Kingdom of Christ and oppose His teachings. But, they also opposed these vocations specifically because, by their very nature, they often required one to do violence against another person, or even to take another human's life—both of which are forbidden by Christ's teachings. In other words, if we are going to take seriously the command to love our

neighbor as we have been loved by God, that probably means we shouldn't kill them, or use violence against them.

Still, I know this is a nuanced topic and many of us are very sensitive about this because we have a son, or a daughter, or a father or a brother, or a mother, etc., who has served or is serving in the military or with the police force; or we ourselves have done so. This is especially difficult if our loved ones have died in the course of performing their duties as soldiers or police officers.

So, having acknowledged this, let me first of all say that everyone and anyone is forgiven by God, no matter what they've done in their past. Jesus always responded to everyone he met with forgiveness, even if they didn't ask for it; and in fact almost no one ever did ask for it. Jesus automatically responds with "Your sins are forgiven" no matter who he engages with, or what their chosen profession or experience may have been.

> WHETHER A PROSTITUTE, OR A SOLDIER, OR A ZEALOT, OR A TAX COLLECTOR, OR EVEN A ROMAN SOLDIER NAILING HIM TO A CROSS, JESUS FORGIVES; AT ALL TIMES AND IN EVERY WAY.

Whether a prostitute, or a soldier, or a zealot, or a tax collector, or even a Roman soldier nailing him to a cross, Jesus forgives; at all times and in every way. So, let's take any guilt or shame or fear off the table before we go any further. No soldier, or police officer, or anyone who has served in the military or with a police force is condemned for having done so.

What I hope to communicate in this book is that Jesus calls us to engage in the pursuit of peace rather than participate in violence. We have been given a ministry of reconciliation, not conflict. Our calling is to something closer to the path of Christ who shows us a better way to live by loving our enemies rather than killing them.

As we've already seen, those who walk in the path of the Messiah must decide for themselves to relinquish their need for weapons. It's not something they are coerced into doing by someone else. Rather, because they see the wisdom of loving rather than fighting, they choose to lay down their arms of war and embrace the "other" with arms of love. No one can make this decision for you. Either you are convinced that walking in this path of peace is something you truly desire to do, or not. If not, there's no condemnation for you. But, one should consider whatever path one is walking on and take time to think about where this path is leading. Is it a path that leads to peace, or reconciliation or life? Or, is it a path that leads to conflict, violence, or death?

I realize you may not see it as black and white as I'm describing it. Fair enough. That's for you to decide. My goal, as I've said, is simply to point out these verses and illuminate Church history to show you how these concepts were first communicated and how these ideas were originally formed by those who followed Jesus. The rest is up to you.

What if I'm in the military now?
I have several good friends who currently serve in the military. If that's you, my advice would be to seriously consider your situation and prayerfully ask God if this is where you belong or not. And I make no assumptions in advance about what the answer you receive might be. It's entirely possible that God might tell you to remain exactly where you are. If so, continue to serve in whatever capacity you're in without shame. However, if you sincerely ask God this question and the response is to walk away, there are options. Several people I know have successfully applied for a Conscientious Objector discharge from the military.

One friend of mine was National Merit scholarship recipient Mike Izbicki, a 25 year old man who served aboard a U.S .Navy submarine. After reading the Gospel of Matthew and the Sermon on the Mount he decided that he could not, in good conscience, launch a nuclear missile if ordered to do so. His request was denied—twice—before he was eventually granted the discharge, but in doing so he earned a peace of heart and mind that he so desperately needed. "I was uneasy over the frankness with which people talked about killing," he said. "I realized that I could not be responsible for killing anyone."[54]

However, several friends of mine have also prayed this way and determined that God's heart was for them to remain where they are. One friend is a commander who has become a sort of surrogate father and older brother to many of the men and women under his command. He takes the time to listen to them, encourage them, pray with them, and even point them—whenever possible—to the love of Christ. Both of my friends are doing exactly what God has called them to do. Neither of them is condemned for their actions, and if you're where you're supposed to be, neither are you.

What if I used to be in the military? Now what?

I know several Christian men and women who have served in military conflict in the past and regret what they've done in the name of God and country. If that's you, I'd say as I've said above that you are loved and forgiven for whatever past mistakes you may have made, whether serving in the military or otherwise. God's forgiveness is absolute. God's love endures forever. You are not condemned by God for the violence you may have participated in. Of course, this doesn't mean you can necessarily forgive yourself so easily.

> YOU ARE GOD'S CHILD AND NOTHING WILL EVER SEPARATE YOU FROM GOD'S LOVE. NOTHING.

Often this inner healing takes a bit longer to process. You may even want to seek out a good, licensed therapist who can help you navigate the pain and trauma associated with the effects of engaging in violent conflict. But, as you do so, please keep in mind that there is nothing but grace and forgiveness for you as far as God is concerned. You are God's child and nothing will ever separate you from God's love. Nothing.

What about being a police officer? Is that okay?
Many who decide to serve as a police officer do so because of a sincere desire to help others. They take very seriously the motto "To Protect and Serve" and enter into this profession from a place of humility. However, some people who join the police force do so out of an inner desire to have power over other people. That's not just my opinion. Studies have been done that show an overwhelming number of police officers exhibit disturbing narcissistic and violent tendencies.[55] Carrying a badge and a gun makes them feel powerful, and this often leads to an abuse of that power over those who cannot fight back. Obviously, if you're serving as a police officer as a way to scratch an itch for dominating other people and boosting your fragile ego, this isn't the best profession for you and you might need to seek counseling for that. However, if you're someone who genuinely desires to help people rather than hurt them, there are a few considerations to examine. First, if you're not yet a police officer, have you talked to anyone who currently serves in this capacity? Are they someone who exhibits the loving, gentle and humble character of Christ? If so, ask them how serving as a police officer hurts or hinders their walk with Jesus. Are they glad they chose this profession or do they wish they had chosen another path? If they do find ways to operate as a police officer without compromising their sincere devotion to Christ, ask them how they do it. What are the challenges? How do they cope with the extreme levels of human depravity and violence they encounter on a daily basis? Do they go to a counselor? Are they practicing any spiritual

disciplines that enable them to survive the rigors of police work? These are the sorts of questions you should have answered before you decide to become a police officer. If you can't find anyone who exhibits these characteristics or who can honestly answer these sorts of questions for you, there may be a very good reason why. If you do find someone, and if they answer these questions satisfactorily for you, then and only then should you seriously consider such a profession in law enforcement.

How do we define "violence"? Is it any use of force? What about if I use force to push my child out of the street when a bus is coming? Is that wrong? Where do we draw the line?
In nearly every case where I've been engaged in dialog with another Christian about the question of nonviolence this question has come up: "But how do we define 'violence'?" So, let's take a moment to answer this one now. First of all, I'm not sure that most of us really don't understand violence when we see it. When Jesus tells us not to respond to violence with violence, what do we think he means? We certainly know violence when someone uses it against us, don't we? This is exactly what is meant by the term "using violence", then. Whatever harmful action someone takes against you is the very thing you should not use against another person. Do we need to create a bullet list of what qualifies as "violence" and what does not? Often someone will point out that a surgeon who uses a scalpel to cut into a patient in order to remove a tumor might be accused of using violence. But, have you ever talked that way? Do you know of anyone who complained about the "violence" of doctors who perform surgery on their patients? I can't say that I have ever been in any conversations where such terminology was used. Violence can take many forms. Sometimes because we love someone we may push them out of the path of an approach vehicle. Is that

violence? Well, let's see … are we doing this to harm them? Obviously not. So, this is not the sort of violence that Jesus is forbidding his followers to engage in. When Jesus urges us to refrain from violence it's so that we can take another path that leads to life and the well-being of the "other." In situations where we feel the very strong urge to respond to violence with violence, this is where Jesus wants us to stop and reconsider our options. As we've already discussed elsewhere, when we take time to respond to violence with acts of love and compassion, the

> WHEN WE RESPOND TO HATE WITH LOVE, THIS IS AN OPPORTUNITY FOR TRANSFORMATION TO TAKE PLACE—BOTH IN THE OTHER PERSON AND IN US, AS WELL.

glorious Kingdom of God breaks into the situation. When we respond to hate with love, this is an opportunity for transformation to take place—both in the other person and in us, as well.

Can Nonviolence Stop Active Shooters?

It's probably unfair to accuse those who practice nonviolence of being unable to stop an active shooter. Especially when those are the very situations that are only initiated by embracing the philosophy of redemptive violence—or simply violence in general—as a means to an end. Once there's an active shooter in your building, it's too late to ask the nonviolent practitioners to step in and fix the problem. Because the problem was created by those who specifically reject nonviolence in the first place. As long as we continue to live in a society that puts its trust in the power of violence and a show of force to keep the peace, we will always have to suffer more violence at the hands of those who have been raised within such a society.

Nonviolence is very effective, however, in preventing these sorts of active shooter events. In other words, the more we embrace and teach and model creative nonviolence, the more opportunity for avoiding violence in the first place.

What if an intruder breaks into my home and holds a gun to my child's/spouse's head?

Easily the most common "what if" question I've ever heard in all of my years talking with Christians about Jesus's commands to love our enemies is this one. In this imaginary scenario, the assumed options are either to do absolutely nothing or to go fort he headshot and blow the other guy's brains out. But there are several problems with this. Firstly, that what Jesus wants us to do is "absolutely nothing" in these situations. Somehow when he says, "Do not resist an evil person" or "Love your enemies" what they hear is, "Just sit there and let people walk all over you." But, as we've already seen, to obey Jesus's commands to walk in this path, the one thing we can never do is "nothing at all." On the contrary, to follow Jesus in this path means doing even more than we could possibly imagine. In several real-life versions of this "gun-to-the-head" type scenario, there have been examples where Jesus-followers responded by praying for the gunman, singing worship songs until the person left the house, making the person something to eat, pouring them a glass of wine, laughing hysterically until the person fled the scene, rebuking the person in the name of Jesus until they ran outside, and an essentially endless array of other things that all "worked" to disarm or confuse the attacker without doing them any harm through violence.[56] In other words, use your imagination.

> LET'S IMAGINE THAT INSTEAD OF A STRANGER HOLDING THE GUN TO YOUR WIFE'S HEAD IT WAS YOUR OWN SON OR DAUGHTER. NOW WHAT? WOULD YOU BE SO QUICK TO PULL THE TRIGGER?

Secondly, in this scenario above the other assumption is that only one of those people—the loved one—is worth saving and protecting. The intruder's life means nothing, apparently. But, let's imagine that instead of a stranger holding the gun to your wife's head it was your own son or daughter. Now what? Would you be so quick to pull the trigger? Or would you suddenly decide to lay down your weapon and look for any and all possible solutions that protected and preserved the lives of everyone involved? If so, you're now thinking the way Jesus wants you to because you're learning the wisdom of what it means to love— not only those who love you in return but to love even those who hate you and mistreat you and abuse you. As a reminder, his statement was:

> "If you love those who love you, what credit is that to you? Even sinners love those who love them. And if you do good to those who are good to you, what credit is that to you? Even sinners do that. And if you lend to those from whom you expect repayment, what credit is that to you? Even sinners lend to sinners, expecting to be repaid in full. But love your enemies, do good to them, and lend to them without expecting to get anything back. Then your reward will be great, and you will be children of the Most High, because he is kind to the ungrateful and wicked. Be merciful, just as your Father is merciful." (Luke 6:32-36)

So, if we shoot the intruder dead, we are simply living by the common rule "love those who love you back" and, according to Jesus, there is nothing special about that. Instead, Jesus urges us to love more, not less. He calls us to enlarge our circle of love to include those who have never been loved the way we have. Our mission is to become ambassadors of this kind of self-giving love so that those who have never experienced it might have an opportunity to become transformed by it.

Another option for us in these sorts of situations is simply to insert ourselves between the victim and the attacker. Yes, we may die in the process, but, again, our death might lead to more beautiful outcomes for the perpetrator and create a more beautiful legacy of transformation for that person.

A friend of mine, Rick Pidcock, recently wrote about a real-life encounter with an intruder in his home that's worth recounting here:

> "When my wife was 38 weeks pregnant, I woke up one night to hands touching my feet. Initially, I assumed it was my wife walking through the dark. But then I turned to my left and noticed that she was still in bed with me. When I looked back to the foot of my bed, there was the outline of a man staring down at us. I lunged at him while yelling for my wife to turn on the lights. And when she did, we saw that the man had stripped down to his underwear. Two days later when the intruder knocked on our door to apologize after being released by the police, I told him, "If I had a gun, you could have died."[57]

So, one must also consider the possibility of not owning a weapon in the first place. As someone who once owned several guns, I can now honestly say that I do not own a gun and since there are none in my home the chances of me shooting someone who breaks in to harm me are exactly zero. But, this is a conscious decision I made a long time ago. This means we might have to make up our minds to take deadly force off the table far in advance so that taking another person's life isn't really an option for us.

CHAPTER 10

NEW EVIDENCE: EARLY CHRISTIAN SOLDIERS?

"The church does not have an alternative to war. The church is the alternative to war."

— STANLEY HAUERWAS

As I was heading into the second Pacifist Fight Club event, several years ago, I received an email with links to an article which claimed that my position regarding the non-participation of the early Christian church in the military was inaccurate.

The main piece of evidence supplied to me at that time was the discovery of an historical (second century) document which detailed the actions of several Christians who were part of the army of Marcus Aurelius. Second to that was a response by Tertullian (a second century church father) who claimed that the prayers of those Christian soldiers were instrumental in the victory of that army.

Since our event was only a few days away, I shared it with fellow presenter Thomas Crisp and we both did mention this evidence briefly during the discussion sessions following the presentations, but at the time we had no good response for this baffling challenge to our claim that no early Christians ever participated in violence prior to the emergence of the Emperor Constantine.

A few months later, my dear friend Herb Montgomery contacted me because he had come across this same information and, like myself, was a bit crest-fallen to have discovered evidence that suggested the early Christian church actually *did* participate in military actions much earlier than we had come to believe.

I shared the research I had done up to that point with him and we corresponded a little back and forth. As a result of Herb's continued research there is much to discuss regarding this apparent contradiction between Christian pacifists and those Christians who hold to redemptive justice.

Here's a little more background information and a summary of what we found—and by "we" I mostly mean the diligence of my friend, Herb Montgomery.

THE RAIN SOLDIERS

The event which informs this discussion occurred when Roman General Marcus Aurelius was preparing to go to battle with barbarian forces in what we now call Germany. His men were exhausted and suffering from heat exposure. The forces ahead of them were fresh and they were outnumbered. After praying to his own pagan gods (and finding no help), Marcus summons the Christians in his army and after they pray ("simultaneously") water began to pour from the sky—refreshing them with cool water which they caught and drank from their shields—and pelting the barbarian horde with giant hailstones. As a result, the Romans won the battle.

When I first read of this account it stunned me. I immediately searched online for the source and found only one (a single book) and was immediately skeptical. Mostly because I've been reading about this topic and debating it with people for years and no one has ever (not once) brought up this as evidence that Christians were involved in military service before the time of Constantine.

Keep in mind, the Christian pacifist holds that the early Christian church was anti-war and anti-violence up until the corruption of the church by the Emperor Constantine in the mid 3rd century. How could it be that Christians were engaging in violence so much earlier than this? Well ... hang on a minute and you'll see the whole truth.

I continued to research and I did find an article which backed up the claims of the email and of the book that was quoted. Furthermore, there was a quote by Tertullian who not only referenced the "Rain Soldiers" event but also appeared nonplussed by the fact that Christians were serving in this army.

The quote (taken out of its context, by the way), says:

"You will see this by examining the letters of Marcus Aurelius, that most serious of emperors. For, in his letters, he bears witness that the Germanic drought was removed by the rains obtained through the prayers of *the Christians, who happened to be fighting under him.*" (Tertullian, *Apology.*)

In addition to this, we also have two other quotes by Tertullian referenced which also appear to contradict his many other non-violent, anti-military quotes, for example:

"Looking up to Him [God], we Christians with hands extended ... constantly *beseech Him on behalf of all Emperors. We ask for* them long life, undisturbed power, security at home, *brave armies*, a faithful senate ... "

"*We [Christians]* are sailors along with yourselves; *we serve in the army*; we engage in farming and trading … "

Now, again, you have to remember that Tertullian is the same guy who famously said: *"When Christ disarmed Peter, He disarmed every soldier."*[58]

So, you can see this appears quite contradictory, especially when added to the many, many other anti-military quotes by Tertullian that many Christian Pacifists hold up as evidence that the early followers of Christ did not stand for violence or condone participation in the military.

However, when you peel back the layers and actually read all of the quotes in their entirety what you learn is that, (yes, Virginia), the Christian Pacifists were right all along. For example, when you read Marcus Aurelius' entire epistle regarding this instance what you see is that those Christians in his army were non-combatants. And he even goes further to explain that the reason why they were non-combatants is due to their faith in Christ. Here's the full quote with emphasis on the sections left out by our pro-military friends.

The Epistle of Marcus Aurelius to the Roman Senate reads:

"Having then examined my own position, and my host, with respect to the vast mass of barbarians and of the enemy, I quickly betook myself to prayer to the gods of my country. But being disregarded by them, *I summoned those who among us go by the name of Christians. And having made inquiry, I discovered a great number and vast host of them, and raged against them, which was by no means becoming; for afterwards I learned their power. Wherefore they began the battle, not by preparing weapons, nor arms, nor bugles; for such preparation is hateful to them, on account of the God they bear about in their conscience.* Therefore it is probable that those whom we suppose to be atheists, have God as their ruling power entrenched in their conscience. For having cast themselves on the ground, they prayed not only for me, but also for the whole army as it stood, that they might be delivered from the present thirst and famine. For during five days we had got no water, because there was none; for we were in the heart of Germany, and in the enemy's territory. *And simultaneously with their casting themselves on the ground, and praying to God [a God of whom I am ignorant], water poured from heaven, upon us most refreshingly cool, but upon the enemies of Rome a withering hail. And immediately we recognized the presence of God following on the prayer—a God unconquerable and indestructible.*" (emphasis mine)

The quote continues by arguing for the end to Christian oppression and the punishment of those who persecute them.

If we examine the Tertullian quote in its entirety (without removing all the annoying pacifist bits) we find out that he (believe it or not) was consistently non-violent in his theology.

For context, Tertullian was writing to show the Emperor that Christians were no threat to the Roman government and that they actually prayed for their Emperor as Christ commanded all Christians to do:

"Thither we lift our eyes, with hands outstretched, because free from sin; with head uncovered, for we have nothing whereof to be ashamed; finally, without a monitor, because it is from the heart we supplicate. *Without ceasing, for all our emperors we offer prayer. We pray for life prolonged; for security to the empire; for protection to the imperial house; for brave armies*, a faithful senate, a virtuous people, the world at rest, whatever, as man or Caesar, an emperor would wish. These things I cannot ask from any but the God from whom I know I shall obtain them, both because He alone bestows them and because I have claims upon Him for their gift, as being a servant of His, rendering homage to Him alone, persecuted for His doctrine, offering to Him, at His own requirement, that costly and noble sacrifice of prayer dispatched from the chaste body, an unstained soul, a sanctified spirit, not the few grains of incense a farthing buys—tears of an Arabian tree,—not a few drops of wine,—not the blood of some worthless ox to which death is a relief, and, in addition to other offensive things, a polluted conscience, so that one wonders, when your victims are examined by these vile priests, why the examination is not rather of the sacrificers than the sacrifices. *With our hands thus stretched out and up to God, rend us with your iron claws, hang us up on crosses, wrap us in flames, take our heads from us with the sword, let loose the wild beasts on us, the very attitude of a Christian praying is one of preparation for all punishment. Let this, good rulers be your work: wring from us the soul, beseeching God on the emperor's behalf."*[59]

See that? Tertullian is saying that Christians are praying for God to bless their Emperor even while they are being tortured and killed for their faith. This sounds more like the Tertullian that Christian Pacifists know and love.

Many have tried to say that Tertullian and Origen were not against military involvement because of any non-violent Christian pacifism but mainly because of the participation in pagan rituals and swearing allegiance to the Roman Emperor as a Deity. However, the following quote from Tertullian demolishes that argument soundly:

> *"I think we must first inquire whether warfare is proper at all for Christians.* What sense is there in discussing the merely accidental, when that on which it rests is to be condemned? Do we believe it lawful for a human oath to be superadded to one divine, for a man to come under promise to another master after Christ, and to abjure father, mother, and all nearest kinsfolk, whom even the law has commanded us to honour and love next to God Himself, to whom the Gospel, too, holding them only of less account than Christ, has in like manner rendered honour? *Shall it be held lawful to make an occupation of the sword, when the Lord proclaims that he who uses the sword shall perish by the sword? And shall the son of peace take part in the battle when it does not become him even to sue at law? And shall he apply the chain, and the prison, and the torture, and the punishment, who is not the avenger even of his own wrongs?"* ...
> Touching this primary aspect of the question, as to the unlawfulness even of a military life itself, I shall not add more, that

the secondary question may be restored to its place. *Indeed, if, putting my strength to the question, I banish from us the military life ... "*[60]

So, it's fairly clear that Tertullian did not want any follower of Christ to engage in military action or warfare and that his reasons were directly related to obedience towards Christ's commands against using violence. In this same work, he also argues that:

> *"Of course, if faith comes later, and finds any preoccupied with military service ...* when a man [already in the military] has become a believer, and faith has been sealed, *there must be either an immediate abandonment of it* [military service], *which has been the course with many,* or all sorts of quibbling will have to be resorted to in order to avoid offending God, and that is not allowed even outside of military service;"[61] (emphasis mine)

In this document, Tertullian urges those who are already serving in the military to cease involvement and, if necessary, suffer a martyrs death (as was often the case).

Finally, let's end with a look at how Tertullian handles the common objection we often hear from pro-military Christians regarding the Old Testament use and acceptance of warfare as an argument for why Christians should be free to go to war today:

> *"But now inquiry is made about this point, whether a believer may turn himself unto military service,* and whether the military may be admitted unto the faith, even the rank and file, or each inferior grade, to whom there is no necessity for taking part in sacrifices or capital punishments *(Note:* he's talking about an exception whereby a Christian in the military might not have to take the offensive oaths to Caesar as "Lord and Savior", etc.). *There is no agreement between the divine and the human sacrament, the standard of Christ and the standard of the devil, the camp of light and the camp of darkness. One soul cannot be due to two masters— God and Cæsar. And yet Moses carried a rod, and Aaron wore a buckle, and John [Baptist] is girt with leather and Joshua the son of Nun leads a line of march; and the People warred: if it pleases*

you to sport with the subject. (Sound familiar?) *But how will a Christian man war, nay, how will he serve even in peace, without a sword, which the Lord has taken away?* For albeit soldiers had come unto John, and had received the formula of their rule; albeit, likewise, a centurion had believed; *still the Lord afterward, in disarming Peter, disarmed every soldier.*"[62]

So, in spite of so-called "evidence" that appears to contradict the claim that the early Church was peaceful and non-violent, the truth is still evident: The followers of Jesus did not approve of warfare nor engage in violence until the time of Constantine in the mid third century.

THE FOLLOWERS OF JESUS DID NOT APPROVE OF WARFARE NOR ENGAGE IN VIOLENCE UNTIL THE TIME OF CONSTANTINE IN THE MID THIRD CENTURY.

For those of us who desire to follow Christ with all our hearts, we cannot appeal to the Old Testament to support a belief in redemptive violence. At the very heart of this issue is one single fact: Jesus compels us to love our enemies, do good to those who hate us, and bless those who curse us. He disarmed Peter and he forbid His disciples to work violence against others. We cannot serve both God and Caesar.[63]

CHAPTER 11

GIVING UP MY X-BOX FOR GANDHI

"We are constantly being astonished these days at the amazing discoveries in the field of violence. But I maintain that far more undreamt of and seemingly impossible discoveries will be made in the field of nonviolence."

— GANDHI[64]

In my own personal journey into this path of preemptive love and creative nonviolence, I've had to wrestle with a few things about myself that I didn't anticipate at first.

For example, I had studied the Sermon on the Mount for nearly a decade by the time I was in my thirties, and I had started this little group called "Pacifist Fight Club" which spun out into actual conferences where people would come to hear messages about nonviolence and listen to testimonies from actual soldiers who had left the military under the conscientious objector rule, and I had written dozens of articles about why Christians needed to take the nonviolent teachings of Jesus seriously. I kinda thought I had this whole nonviolent enemy-loving thing down cold. But, then I started reading a book that my friend, Professor Thomas Crisp, had recommended to me which was a collection of letters from Gandhi. I looked it up, ordered a copy and started reading it a few weeks later. At first, it was pretty much what I expected. Great quotes, plenty of thoughts to underline, almost every other page dog-eared for later reference. But then I came across a section that really made me stop and think about this nonviolence thing in a totally different way.

First, the idea that nonviolence was rooted in the very fabric of the Kingdom of God: *"My experience tells me that the Kingdom of God is within us, and that we can realize it not by saying, 'Lord, Lord,' but by doing God's will and God's work."*[65] This simple quote, in context, really made me stop and consider how the ethic of nonviolence is something that must be deeply internalized. Not merely a set of beliefs or even conditioned practices where we go through the motions, but an inner reality that permeates our entire being.

Then, I read another quote that really started to clarify this concept for me a bit further: *"If one does not practice nonviolence in one's personal relations with others and hopes to use it in bigger affairs, one is vastly mistaken. Nonviolence, like charity, must begin at home ... one cannot be nonviolent in one's own circle and violent outside it. Or else, one is not truly nonviolent, even in one's own circle."*[66]

This really stirred something inside of me. I started to realize how much I not only tolerated my own inner violence, but how I also amused myself with violence in the form of entertainment, and especially in the form of video games.

I really want to stress that this is not something I would ever hold against another person. This was totally a personal conviction brought about as I began to consider just what my devotion to Christlike nonviolence really meant for me. If I was sincerely convinced that Jesus calls us into a new way of seeing and being human without violence, then why was I not uncomfortable turning on my X-box to play violent video games for several hours at a time? I rationalized that this was my way of relaxing, blowing off steam, destressing after a long day of work, etc. But, once I really began to evaluate myself, I realized that I was much more accepting of violence as a solution—even to imaginary problems—than I was previously willing to admit. After a few weeks of mulling this over, I decided to stop playing video games completely. Not because I saw it as something bad or evil, per se, but because I had begun to realize just how much my exposure to those violent images and actions had compromised my commitment to follow Jesus into a lifestyle of genuine love for others.

> ONCE I REALLY BEGAN TO EVALUATE MYSELF, I REALIZED THAT I WAS MUCH MORE ACCEPTING OF VIOLENCE AS A SOLUTION—EVEN TO IMAGINARY PROBLEMS—THAN I WAS PREVIOUSLY WILLING TO ADMIT.

Before you accuse me of following Gandhi rather than Jesus, let me assure you that, for all of his many other personal flaws and failures, Gandhi had a very sincere admiration for, respect for, and love for Jesus. He not only read and tried to follow the Sermon on the Mount on a daily basis for the latter part of his life, he also wrote many beautiful and surprising things about Jesus. For example:

"Jesus expressed, as no other could, the spirit and will of God. It is in this sense that I see him and recognize him as the Son of God. And because the life of Jesus has the significance and the transcendancy to which I have alluded, I believe that he belongs not solely to Christianity, but to the entire world, to all races and people."

"I consider Western Christianity in its practical working a negation of Christ's Christianity. I cannot conceive Jesus, if he was living in the flesh in our midst, approving of modern Christian organizations, public worship, or modern ministry. If Christians would simply cling to the Sermon on the Mount, which was delivered not merely to the peaceful disciples but a groaning world, they would not go wrong ... "[67]

"The ministry of Jesus lasted only for three brief years. His teaching was misunderstood even during his own time, and today's Christianity is a denial of his central teaching, 'Love your enemy' ... But it is not a thing to be grasped by mere intellect, it must sink into our hearts."[68]

This idea of allowing the nonviolent, enemy-loving teachings of Jesus to sink down into our hearts until it saturates our thoughts, changes our hearts, and transforms our inner being is really what matters most, I believe. If these ideas remain mere philosophies then our nonviolent actions are ultimately useless and are of no real value to anyone—even to ourselves. Because, unless we are so filled with the love of Christ that it permeates to our very soul, we are not yet the sincere ambassadors of love, or of reconciliation that Christ intends us to be.

UNLESS WE ARE SO FILLED WITH THE LOVE OF CHRIST THAT IT PERMEATES TO OUR VERY SOUL, WE ARE NOT YET THE SINCERE AMBASSADORS OF LOVE, OR OF RECONCILIATION THAT CHRIST INTENDS US TO BE.

Again, this isn't about pointing the finger at anyone else. It's more about taking personal stock of our own souls to determine whether or not we have been—or are being—truly transformed by the love of Christ from the inside out. Not everyone will find they need to give away their X-Box or give up violent video games to stay true to the path that Jesus has laid out for them. Some may find their struggles with inner violence lead them to very different conclusions, and that's perfectly acceptable. The goal is not to impose any restrictions on other people artificially. In my case, no one came to me and told me to do this, or to stop that. Not even Gandhi's letters did that for me. But, as I read those letters, the Holy Spirit did point out some things that were very necessary for me to stay on this path of loving nonviolence.

Perhaps the point is that this is a journey. It's something that changes you as you walk the path. In fact, I've heard it said that there is no path to nonviolence, but that nonviolence is the path. Or was it this?

"There is no way to peace. Peace is the way." (Gandhi)

The more we walk this path of peace, the more we experience this inner transformation within. We may not immediately become convinced that we should study war no more. We might not begin our journey by beating our weapons into garden tools. But, if we are on the path at all, we may eventually find ourselves becoming convinced that this Prince of Peace was really on to something. We might decide to invest a little more of ourselves into this way of love, and as we continue following this road, we are sure to reach that milestone where that old way of thinking, and living, and behaving, just doesn't feel right to us anymore. Maybe that's when we'll look down at these symbols of violence and decide we have no more use for them anymore. That's the day when we take out the trash, clean out our closets, and unburden ourselves of all of those useless, outdated, and worthless reminders of that old way of thinking.

CHAPTER 12

SOLA CHRISTUS

"One day we must come to see that peace is not merely a distant goal that we seek, but that it is a means by which we arrive at that goal. We must pursue peaceful ends through peaceful means."

— MARTIN LUTHER KING, JR.

"The application of Jesus' teaching to his social world is also seen in the fact that his movement was the peace party within Palestine."

— MARCUS BORG

For many of us, the very fact that we were born into a Christian home in the United States of America nearly guarantees that we will never fully embrace the nonviolent, enemy-loving teachings of Jesus. We've just got too much to overcome to actually shed our rights and lay aside our freedoms for the sake of Christ.

Our nation was born and bred in the dark red womb of violence. From the days when the earliest colonists from England killed Native Americans for their land and resources, to when those same Christian Colonists put other Christians to death for preaching the wrong Gospel, violence has been our legacy from the very beginning.

When other nations ended the practice of slavery through boycotts, prayer vigils and legislation, our nation turned to violence to settle the issue. In fact, there's almost nothing we've ever accomplished as a nation apart from the implementation of violence in some form or the other. You might say we don't know any other way to solve our problems. Even though, ironically, so many among us want to claim Christ as our National mascot, we completely ignore his teachings when it comes to how we actually live our lives.

> SADLY, I BELIEVE WE MUST ADMIT THAT AMERICAN CHRISTIANITY IS A CHRISTLESS CHRISTIANITY.

Sadly, I believe we must admit that American Christianity is a Christless Christianity. We demand the Ten Commandments to be displayed in our courthouses, but we never give a thought to Jesus's Sermon on the Mount.

We justify our cruelty to immigrants by quoting random passages from Paul's letter to the Romans, but skip over dozens of commands from Jesus about showing mercy, caring for the weak and vulnerable, and totally ignore his warning that "whatever you have done for the least of these, you have done it to me."

We cry out for "an eye for an eye and a tooth for a tooth" to be our standard for justice, but ignore the fact that Jesus specifically corrected this teaching by calling us to respond with love.

In other words, Jesus wanted his followers to endure injustice and to take those moments as opportunities to put the extravagant love of Christ's Kingdom into practice. He wanted us to allow the heart of God to shine forth into the darkness and dazzle the eyes of those who have never seen or even imagined such overwhelming love could exist.

This is how we change the world. This is how we transform our enemies into friends. This is how we end the violence. This is how we push back the darkness—not with more darkness—but with true, undeniable light; the light that only comes from God.

If the best we can do is take an eye for an eye, we will never escape this world of blindness. If the best we can do is to continue to behave exactly the way we would had Christ never come and spoken these words of life to us, we will never experience freedom. But this is not the best we can do. Not by a longshot.

We can stop and reconsider all of this. We can think differently. We can at least try to follow the words of Jesus, if for no other reason than it's the one thing we have yet to actually try.

All other attempts to change the world have failed. All other avenues have long been exhausted. What if we try to love one another as Christ has loved us? What if we consider others better than ourselves? What if we refuse to regard others from a worldly point of view? What if we tried to put Christ back in our Christianity? Honestly, at this point, I wonder what have we got to lose?

After all, our world is on fire. We can't escape the images of hate on our screens. We can't ignore the violence on our streets. We can't pretend we're not broken in profoundly deep ways. Not anymore.

Our news cycles are filled with examples of people who identify as Christians but use deadly force against their enemies. Our unwavering faith in the myth of redemptive violence is slowly killing us. Our reflex—as it has always been—is to continually reach for the same familiar solutions that have failed us time and time again. When we're attacked, we fight back. When we're threatened we reach for our guns. Violence is our answer. We still believe that if we could just kill enough bad people we can make the world a better place. But, even so, if we're honest, we already know deep down inside that those solutions will fail us again. Why? Because they are simply incapable of changing the real problem: *Us.*

Yes, we are the problem. Our fears are the fuel to these flames we are now surrounded by. Our need for power is what drives our descent into this quagmire we're in today. These old solutions will not work. They've never worked before. They won't work now.

Passing laws won't change this. Gaining political advantage won't accomplish anything but more of the same. There are no politicians out there with the answer. There are no candidates coming to save us. There are no policies to heal this deep wound of ours.

> THERE ARE NO POLITICIANS OUT THERE WITH THE ANSWER. THERE ARE NO CANDIDATES COMING TO SAVE US. THERE ARE NO POLICIES TO HEAL THIS DEEP WOUND OF OURS.

The definition of insanity is doing the same thing over and over again, expecting a different result. Redemptive violence does not work. War is not a solution. To experience something different, we'll have to try something we've never tried before. All of our efforts so far have been focused on turning off the darkness. But no one can do that. The darkness cannot be contained, managed or legislated. The only way to remove the darkness is to turn on the light.

So, what if Jesus was right about what's wrong with us? What if he knew that our fears would lead us exactly here? What if he knew that hating our enemies would only lead to more violence? What if he could see the way out of this never-ending cycle of "us vs them"? I believe he did.

We've been playing the "eye for an eye" game for centuries. It's gotten us exactly here where we are today. If we continue to fight fire with fire we'll only create a larger fire that is even now threatening to consume us all.

So, what if we did something totally different? Rather than do the things we always do and have always done, what if tried something completely unexpected? *What if we loved our enemies? What if we blessed them? What if tried to overcome evil with good?* Isn't this what love does? Doesn't love cast out all fear?

Yes, I believe it does. Because, just as the light was made to dispel the darkness, love was made to cast out fear. Mercy triumphs over judgment, and justice is a river that flows and cannot be stopped.

I believe Jesus offers us an opportunity to walk a better path; one that leads away from violence; one that leads us towards healing, and reconciliation, and life. What's missing are people willing to walk this path. We already know that what we're doing now—and what we have always done—leads us exactly here.

If we don't like where we are now, we'll need to try walking a different path. The Gospel of Christ transforms all of us - even our enemies - into new creatures with new hearts dedicated to justice, committed to peace, resolved to service, devoted to love.

This means we sincerely desire the redemption of those who kneel down on the necks of other human beings and take their lives away. We rejoice when they are set free from the blindness that made them forget the humanity of everyone, the brotherhood of all mankind. We weep with them when they recognize the horrific things they've done; when they realize they have murdered their own brothers and sisters; when they understand that the mercy they are offered is bestowed at the highest price; when we all understand that the salvation of the worst of us is necessary for the salvation of all of us, and the grace that we give is the grace that we need ourselves more than anything else.

Jesus has illuminated the path of peace for us. He's shown us how to study war no more. He's demonstrated how to love our enemies, bless those who curse us, pray for those who hate us, and overcome evil with good. Now that we know the things that make for peace, will we turn around and walk in this path?

We can't turn off the darkness. We should know this by now. Our only hope is to turn on the light. Our only hope is to love the fear away. Our only hope is to try what we have never tried before. This world will never change until we change.

Let the transformation begin.

FINAL THOUGHTS ON FOLLOWING JESUS

"We have grasped the mystery of the atom and rejected the Sermon on the Mount. The world has achieved brilliance without conscience. Ours is a world of nuclear giants and ethical infants. We know more about war than we know about peace, more about killing than we know about living. If we continue to develop our technology without wisdom or prudence, our servant may prove to be our executioner."

— GENERAL OMAR BRADLEY, ARMISTICE DAY SPEECH, NOV. 11, 1948

This book you're holding in your hand is the final one in a series I started writing a little over 5 years ago. Throughout this series, I have done my best to peel away the man-made layers of political entanglement, toxic theology, hierarchical manipulation, end-times hysteria, scriptural corruption, and twisted religiosity that have been allowed to obscure the face of Jesus over the last two thousand years. Like a tangled overgrowth of stubborn vines that have spread unchecked for way too long, the various doctrines and theories of a few Christian men have held the Bride of Christ immobile; paralyzed and blinded to the true and beautiful face of Jesus of Nazareth.

On the one hand, I wish it had not been necessary to write these seven books at all. In a perfect world, the people who knew Jesus best would have made sure to pass along the simplicity of his message, and the purity of his love, one person at a time, and protected the beautiful Gospel of love, and of Christ in us, without fail. Oh, they did a wonderful job, for the most part, in those first two or three hundred years or so. Somehow even the original disciples went back on their calling to wash feet and wait tables, opting instead to assume titles like "teacher" and "pastor" and "bishop," almost from the very beginning. About the same time they started pushing the women to the side, or back into the kitchen to make sandwiches for the men who did most of the public ministry. We at least have some references to these amazing women who helped form the earliest Christian communities in the writings of the Apostle Paul, and from Jesus, of course. We see them serving as deacons, elders, prophets, evangelists, teachers, pastors and yes, even as apostles, in the pages of the New Testament. But, sadly, almost within a generation or two, Christian leaders were exclusively male and wrote horrible things about women that are too offensive for me to even repeat here in this book.

Still, we do see a strong thread of Christlike enemy-love and compassionate nonviolence being practiced throughout this turbulent season of the early Church. For nearly 300 years they resisted evil with good, and refused to take up arms against their oppressor. In fact, they are the largest community of Christians in all of human history who could truthfully claim to have beaten their swords into plowshares to study war no more. Theirs was a truly Christlike community of love in the face of unspeakable evil. Suffering at the hands of cruel emperors like Nero, Diocletian, and others who went out of their way to torture, humiliate and crush them into obscurity. They overcame that evil with love. They resisted this hatred with genuine humility and breath-taking courage.

However, once these emperors realized this subversive Christ-movement could not be stopped by any other means available, they opted to try another tactic; one that inevitably led those Christ-followers to abandon their devotion to Jesus in exchange for a position of favor within the Empire.

Ever since, the pure face of Jesus has been continually obscured and the beautiful Gospel of Jesus has become harder and harder to hear. Especially when those who claim to follow the Prince of Peace are clinging tightly to their second amendment right to bear arms, and proudly waving the flag of their Empire in their places of worship.

We've come a long way since those days of simple devotion to the way of Jesus, haven't we? Some may even suggest that we've strayed a bit too far off course. This is why, for me, writing these books has been so very necessary. Because I feel like we've lost our way and need to find our way back to that original path that Jesus laid out for us so long ago.

What's more, I'm concerned about what's at stake if we fail to rediscover the beautiful gospel of Jesus in our time. We're already so far from that simple path of loving God and loving one another as Jesus loved

RATHER THAN BECOMING THE LIGHT OF THE WORLD THAT PROVIDES HOPE AND COMFORT FOR THE OUTCAST AND THE BROKEN, WE'RE STANDING ON THE SIDE OF THOSE IN POWER, CONDEMNING THE VERY SORTS OF PEOPLE WHOM JESUS SAID THE KINGDOM BELONGED TO.

us. We're distracted by politics and nationalism. We're dividing over doctrines. We've forgotten our first love. Rather than becoming the light of the world that provides hope and comfort for the outcast and the broken, we're standing on the side of those in power, condemning the very sorts of people whom Jesus said the Kingdom belonged to.

Even worse, the movement inspired by Jesus has become something so foreign to Christ and his message that we've managed to convince people that God is wrathful, vengeful and angry. We've made God into the volcano-god who demands a virgin blood sacrifice before He will even consider accepting us or forgiving us, even though this looks nothing at all like Jesus who told us that if we had seen him, we had seen the Father.

So, what's at stake for us if we don't find our way back to the feet of this original Jesus? Pretty much everything, I'm afraid. At this point, as I see it, we're in an all-or-nothing stage of our faith where we either abandon these toxic, man-made doctrines and theologies and return to the pure, simple gospel of Christ, or the world will continue to suffer. Not that I want to invoke fear. Far from it. I want to inspire hope. I want to show us the way out of the darkness. Because there is always a way out, if we're willing to see it.

I am often accused of being a "Progressive" Christian whenever I speak about following Jesus this way. But, to me, these aren't progressive concepts at all. Rather than being "new" ideas, they are exceptionally "old" ideas that reach back to the little green mount where the son of a carpenter stood up to speak about a different way of living, and pointed us into a path that leads to life, and peace, and joy everlasting.

If anything, I am a "Regressive" Christian who longs for us to return—as much as possible—to a more First Century style of Jesus-Following that involves a sincere devotion to those words of wisdom that turn us upside down and inside out.

So, in these books I've been writing for the last five years, my hope has been to reveal this beautiful Jesus to you. I've tried as hard as I know how to strip away everything that stands between you and him so that his face, his heart and his wisdom can shine as clearly and as brightly as possible. I've done my very best to present this Jesus to you with as little bias as possible.

On the one hand, I'm not sure I've done a very good job. There's so much garbage out there to clear up, so many lies to dispel, so many doctrines to refute. I've majored on those teachings that I've felt were the most destructive to the character of Christ and that did the most harm to his children—Dispensationalism, Penal Substitutionary Atonement, Eternal Conscious Torment, Submission to Hierarchical Authorities, Infallibility and Inerrancy of Scripture, and Political Tribalism—but certainly there are even more filters and screens and prisms that distort the beautiful image of Christ out there. Even in those areas where I've written a book to expose the most toxic distortions of Christ, the problems seem to persist and those who teach these things seem to gain more and more influence over people. It kind of makes me feel as if it was all a bit wasted energy, if I'm being honest. Still, I realize it will take time, and many more voices, to see large scale changes occur.

However, the good news is that I'm encouraged by an almost daily stream of private messages, emails and posts I receive from people who have sincerely experienced freedom from toxic theology due to my books and blog posts. I'm also very relieved to see more and more authors and bloggers and podcasters out there who are taking up the challenge to spread the truly beautiful Gospel of Christ farther and wider than I could ever imagine. All of that gives me a very real hope for the future.

I must also keep in mind that Jesus is entirely capable of making himself known to people without my help. In fact, one could be deeply entangled in every single one of those distorted theologies and—without ever reading a single page of anything I, or anyone else, has ever written—come to one's senses and awaken to the exquisite beauty of Christ all at once. That is sort of what happened to me, I would say. It wasn't one book, or a certain article, or any sort of debate or argument or conversation that led me out of the cold darkness of Evangelical Christianity and into the warm light of the realization of Christ within me. It was, I suppose, the Spirit of God Herself that did all of that. So, while God may or may not use a book, or a song, or a dream, or a film, or some other "inspired" vehicle to introduce Godself to us, the point is that the encounter takes place, and when it does, we are forever transformed.

I have somewhat sarcastically said on more than one occasion that my ministry or purpose in life is to introduce Christians to Jesus. This is probably the best way to express what all of this feels like to me. It's the Christians, I've found, more so than the unbelievers out there, who seem to be the most confused about who Jesus is and what Jesus is like.

IT'S THE CHRISTIANS, I'VE FOUND, MORE SO THAN THE UNBELIEVERS OUT THERE, WHO SEEM TO BE THE MOST CONFUSED ABOUT WHO JESUS IS AND WHAT JESUS IS LIKE.

Surprisingly, the majority of the unbelievers and non-Christians I've known are usually not as resistant to the notion that Jesus was a nonviolent, enemy-loving Messiah who taught us to love God and love our neighbors as we have been loved ourselves.

So, this is where I've felt called to focus my attention for the last two decades. I hope it's doing some good. I suppose I will never completely know just where these books end up or how they will be perceived in the years to come.

For now, my greatest hope is that they have been a blessing to you, dear friend. I hope you have experienced more of the love of Jesus after reading my books. I hope you have a deeper connection to Christ than you did at the start. If so, then I am very grateful and that has made everything worthwhile.

At least, this is my prayer. Let our Jesus be untangled, unbound, unveiled, unexpected, undefeated, unforsaken and most of all, may his followers be, like him, unarmed whenever they come into His glorious presence.

From the bottom of my heart, I want to say "Thank you" for reading this book. It has been my honor and privilege to share these thoughts with you. But, be careful. If some of us are courageous enough to start putting this Jesus stuff into practice, it might just change us, and our world, from the inside out.

Wouldn't that be something to see?

HOW TO FIGHT LIKE A CHRISTIAN

While the New Testament on the whole reflects the nonviolent, enemy-loving philosophy of Jesus, we do often come across language that sounds violent, or at least that uses violent imagery as a metaphor for our struggle against temptation evil.

Here are a few of the ways we can learn how to "Fight Like A Christian" without using violence against other people.

KNOW YOUR ENEMY

"Be alert and of sober mind. Your enemy the devil prowls around like a roaring lion looking for someone to devour." (1 Peter 5:8)

UNDERSTAND WHO IS NOT YOUR ENEMY

"For our struggle is not against flesh and blood, but against the rulers, against the authorities, against the powers of this dark world and against the spiritual forces of evil in the heavenly realms." (Eph. 6:12)

KNOW YOUR WEAPONS

"The weapons we fight with are not the weapons of the world. On the contrary, they have divine power to demolish strongholds." (2 Cor. 10:4)

UNDERSTAND YOUR MISSION

"But I tell you, love your enemies and pray for those who persecute you, that you may be children of your Father in heaven." (Matt. 5:44-45)

"But to you who are listening, I say: Love your enemies, do good to those who hate you, bless those who curse you, pray for those who mistreat you. If someone slaps you on one cheek, turn to them the other also. If someone takes your coat, do not withhold your shirt from them." (Luke 6:27-29)

UNDERSTAND THE BATTLE

"If we are distressed, it is for your comfort and salvation; if we are comforted, it is for your comfort, which produces in you patient endurance of the same sufferings we suffer." (2 Cor. 1:6)

BE CONFIDENT

"No weapon formed against you shall prosper" (Isaiah 54:17)

BE SUBVERSIVE

"I am sending you out like sheep among wolves. Therefore, be as shrewd as snakes and as innocent as doves." (Matthew 10:16)

CLAIM THE VICTORY

"…I will build my church, and the gates of Hades will not overcome it." (Matthew 16:18)

SUMMARY

- No human being is your enemy.

- Our "warfare" involves prayer, love, and becoming a blessing to those who hate you.

- Lives may be lost in this battle, and your own life is most certainly one of them.

- If blood must be shed it must be your own.

- You must look out for the well-being of your fellow-soldiers, and your enemy.

- You are a sheep, not a wolf. Trust in your Shepherd for protection.

VERSES OF PEACE FROM THE BIBLE

- "Blessed are the peacemakers, for they will be called children of God." (Matt. 5:9)

- "Have salt in yourselves, and be at peace with one another." (Mark 9:50)

- "But I say to you who hear, Love your enemies, do good to those who hate you" (Luke 6:27)

- "But love your enemies, and do good, and lend, expecting nothing in return, and your reward will be great, and you will be sons of the Most High, for he is kind to the ungrateful and the evil." (Luke 6:35)

- "Repay no one evil for evil, but give thought to do what is honorable in the sight of all." (Romans 12:17)

- "If it is possible, as far as it depends on you, live at peace with everyone." (Romans 12:18)

- "Do not be overcome by evil, but overcome evil with good." (Romans 12:21)

- "For the kingdom of God is not a matter of eating and drinking but of righteousness and peace and joy in the Holy Spirit. Whoever thus serves Christ is acceptable to God and approved by men. So then let us pursue what makes for peace and for mutual upbuilding." (Romans 14:17-19)

- "May the God of hope fill you with all joy and peace in believing, so that by the power of the Holy Spirt you may abound in hope." (Rom. 15:13)

- "Do not repay evil with evil or insult with insult. On the contrary, repay evil with blessing, because to this you were called so that you may inherit a blessing." (1 Peter 3:9)

- "Pursue peace with all people, and holiness, without which no one will see the Lord." (Hebrews 12:14)

- "Make sure that nobody pays back wrong for wrong, but always strive to do what is good for each other and for everyone else." (1 Thess. 5:15)

- "But the wisdom that is from above is first pure, then peaceable, gentle, willing to yield, full of mercy and good fruits, without partiality and without hypocrisy. Now the fruit of righteousness is sown in peace by those who make peace." (James 3:17-18)

- "So whatever you wish that others would do to you, do also to them, for this is the Law and the Prophets." (Matthew 7:12)

- "Be at peace among yourselves." (1 Thess. 5:13)

- "And let the peace of Christ rule in your hearts, to which indeed you were called in one body. And be thankful." (Col. 3:15)

- "And he said to them, "Pay attention to what you hear: with the measure you use, it will be measured to you, and still more will be added to you." (Mark 4:24)

- "I therefore, a prisoner for the Lord, urge you to walk in a manner worthy of the calling to which you have been called, with all humility and gentleness, with patience, bearing with one another in love, eager to maintain the unity of the Spirit in the bond of peace. There is one body and one Spirit—just as you were called to the one hope that belongs to your call— one Lord, one faith, one baptism.." (Eph. 3:1-32)

- "Therefore be imitators of God, as beloved children. And walk in love, as Christ loved us and gave himself up for us, a fragrant offering and sacrifice to God." (Eph. 5:1-2)

- "But the fruit of the Spirit is love, joy, peace, patience, kindness, goodness, faithfulness…" (Gal. 5:22)

- "God has called you to peace." (1 Cor. 7:15)

- "Finally, brothers, rejoice. Aim for restoration, comfort one another, agree with one another, live in peace; and the God of love and peace will be with you." (2 Cor. 3:11)

- "Let him turn away from evil and do good; let him seek peace and pursue it." (1 Peter 3:11)

- "If anyone says, "I love God," and hates his brother, he is a liar; for he who does not love his brother whom he has seen cannot love God whom he has not seen." (1 John 4:20)

- "Let me hear what God the LORD will speak, for he will speak peace to his people…" (Ps. 85:8)

- "Deceit is in the heart of those who devise evil, but those who plan for peace have joy." (Prov. 12:20)

- When a man's ways please the LORD, he makes even his enemies to be at peace with him." (Prov. 16:7)

- "For to us a child is born, to us a son is given; and the government shall be upon his shoulder, and his name shall be called Wonderful Counselor, Mighty God, Everlasting Father, Prince of Peace." (Isaiah 9:6)

EARLY CHURCH FATHERS ON NONVIOLENCE

"We ourselves were well conversant with war, murder, and everything evil, but all of us throughout the whole wide earth have traded in our weapons of war. We have exchanged our swords for ploughshares, our spears for farm tools. Now we cultivate the reverence of God, justice, kindness to men, faith, and the expectation of the future given to us by the Father himself through the Crucified One." – **Justin Martyr (160 AD)** [69]

"If a loud trumpet summons soldiers to war, shall not Christ with a strain of peace issued to the ends of the earth gather up his soldiers of peace? By his own blood and by his word he has assembled an army which sheds no blood in order to give them the Kingdom of Heaven. The trumpet of Christ is his Gospel. He has sounded it and we have heard it. Let us then put on the armour of peace ... The Church is an army of peace which sheds no blood." – **Clement of Alexandria (150-215 AD)** [70]

"The Lord, in disarming Peter, disarmed every soldier." – **Tertullian (160 AD)** [71]

"Christians could never slay their enemies. For the more that kings, rulers, and peoples have persecuted them everywhere, the more Christians have increased in number and grown in strength." – **Origen (184-253 AD)** [72]

"Wherever arms have glittered, they must be banished and exterminated from thence." – **Lactantius (240-320 AD)**[73]

"As simple and quiet sisters, peace and love require no arms. For it is not in war, but in peace, that we are trained." – **Clement of Alexandria (150-215 AD)**[74]

"Above all, Christians are not allowed to correct with violence." – **Clement of Alexandria (150-215 AD)**

"I do not wish to be a king; I am not anxious to be rich; I decline military command ... Die to the world, repudiating the madness that is in it." – **Tatian (120-180 AD)**[75]

"We who formerly used to murder one another now refrain from even making war upon our enemies." – **Justin Martyr (160 AD)**[76]

"Whatever Christians would not wish others to do to them, they do not to others. And they comfort their oppressors and make them their friends; they do good to their enemies. Through love towards their oppressors, they persuade them to become Christians." – **Aristides the Athenian (124 AD)**[77]

"A soldier of the civil authority must be taught not to kill men and to refuse to do so if he is commanded, and to refuse to take an oath. If he is unwilling to comply, he must be rejected for baptism. A military commander or civic magistrate must resign or be rejected. If a believer seeks to become a soldier, he must be rejected, for he has despised God." – **Hippolytus of Rome (170-235 AD)**

"There is nothing better than peace, in which all warfare of things in heaven and things on earth is abolished." – **Ignatius of Antioch (108 AD)**[78]

"The new covenant that brings back peace and the law that gives life have gone forth over the whole earth, as the prophets said: "For out of Zion will go forth the law, and the word of the Lord from Jerusalem; and he will instruct many people; and they will break down their swords into plowshares, and their spears into pruning hooks, and they will no longer learn to make war." These people formed their swords and war lances into plowshares," that is, into instruments used for peaceful purposes. So now, they are unaccustomed to fighting, so when they are struck, they offer also the other cheek." – **Irenaeus (130-202 AD)**

"For since we, a numerous band of men as we are, have learned from His teaching and His laws that evil ought not to be requited with evil, that it is better to suffer wrong than to inflict it, that we would rather shed our own blood than stain our hands and our conscience with that of another. As a result, an ungrateful world is now enjoying–and for a long period has enjoyed–a benefit from Christ. For by his means, the rage of savage ferocity has been softened and has begun to withhold hostile hands from the blood of a fellow creature. In fact, if all men without exception…would lend an ear for a while to his salutary and peaceful rules, … the whole world would be living in the most peaceful tranquility. The world would have turned the use of steel into more peaceful uses and would unite together in blessed harmony."[79] – **Arnobius (330 AD)**

"Those soldiers were filled with wonder and admiration at the grandeur of the man's piety and generosity and were struck with amazement. They felt the force of this example of pity. As a result, many of them were added to the faith of our Lord Jesus Christ and threw off the belt of military service." – **Disputation of Archelaus and Manes**

"We have rejected such spectacles as the Coliseum. How then, when we do not even look on killing lest we should contract guilt and pollution, can we put people to death?" – **Athenagoras of Athens (133-190 AD)** [80]

"How can a man be master of another's life, if he is not even master of his own? Hence he ought to be poor in spirit, and look at Him who for our sake became poor of His own will; let him consider that we are all equal by nature, and not exalt himself impertinently against his own race ... " – **Gregory of Nyssa (335-395 AD)**[81]

"Neither Celsus nor they who think with him are able to point out any act on the part of Christians which savours of rebellion. And yet, if a revolt had led to the formation of the Christian commonwealth, so that it derived its existence in this way from that of the Jews, who were permitted to take up arms in defence of the members of their families, and to slay their enemies, the Christian Lawgiver would not have altogether forbidden the putting of men to death; and yet He nowhere teaches that it is right for His own disciples to offer violence to any one, however wicked." – **Origen (184-253 AD)**[82]

ENDNOTES

INTRODUCTION

1. As reported on Raw Story, Nov. 6, 2017: https://www.rawstory.com/2017/11/watch-trump-loving-pastor-boasts-his-heavily-armed-congregants-would-gun-down-attempted-church-shooters/

2. See Freakonometrics article, "The U.S. Has Been At War 222 Out Of 239 Years" by Arthur Charpentier, 2017, https://freakonometrics.hypotheses.org/50473

3. For more in-depth examination of Rene Girard's Mimetic Theory, please see my book Jesus Unforsaken: Substituting Divine Wrath With Unrelenting Love, chapter 6, pg. 135-150.

CHAPTER 1

4. From An All-Round Ministry, (Charles Spurgeon's Annual Conference Addresses at the Pastors College), "A New Departure." (SIXTEENTH ANNUAL CONFERENCE, Spring 1880)

5. From "Real Time with Bill Maher", May 13, 2011.

6. For more on what the Gospel is and is not, please read my book Jesus Unforsaken: Substituting Divine Wrath With Unrelenting Love.

7. For more on how and why American Christianity has been redefined by political tribalism, see my book Jesus Untangled: Crucifying Our Politics To Pledge Allegiance To The Lamb.

CHAPTER 2

8. As quoted in the book Strength To Love, Martin Luther King, Jr.

CHAPTER 3

9. From Relevant Magazine, issue 24, and online "7 Big Questions" here: http://relevantmagazine.com/god_article.php?id=7418

10. IBID

11. From the essay, The Kingdom of Heaven Suffers Violence: Discerning the Suffering Servant in the Parable of the Wedding Banquet, by Marty Aiken.

CHAPTER 4

12. Note: There is a much longer exploration of this Jesus-Centric approach to the Scriptures available in my book Jesus Unbound: Liberating The Word Of God From The Bible.

13. IBID, David Bercot's closing argument at 1:44:27 https://www.youtube.com/watch?v=K4xQaDDKY7k&list=PLGksKUKUwPqoaQ3OFtpRSwi0g851rs06x&index=17&t=1941s

14. From a personal Facebook post by Rob Grayson.

CHAPTER 5

15. From the book The Good Man Jesus and the Scoundrel Christ by Philip Pullman.

16. From the article: Resisting The Nazis In Various Ways, on July 19, 2017 at OpenDemocracy.net: https://www.opendemocracy.net/en/non-violence-against-nazis-interview-with-george-paxton/

17. IBID.

18. IBID.

19. As detailed in the documentary film, Pray The Devil Back To Hell, 2008.

20. From the lecture at Dartmouth University, "Why Civil Resistance Works: Nonviolence in the Past and Future", https://www.youtube.com/watch?v=EHkzgDOMtYs&t=5s

21. IBID

22. IBID

23. IBID

24. For further study, see Erica Chenoweth's presentation: "Confronting the Myth of the Rational Insurgent" https://www.nakedcapitalism.com/2012/02/erica-chenoweth-confronting-the-myth-of-the-rational-insurgent-2.html

CHAPTER 6

25. As told in the NPR segment "A Victim Treats His Mugger Right", March 28, 2008: https://www.npr.org/2008/03/28/89164759/a-victim-treats-his-mugger-right

26. As told in the NPR podcast Invisibilia, season 2, episode 5, "Disarming A Robbery With A Glass Of Wine": https://www.youtube.com/watch?v=aWseEycdXS8&list=PLGksKUKUwPqrmoR3vWSy-Atk4VPPWZW2P&index=30

27. As told in the CBS News segment "Mother of Amish School Shooter Granted Unexpected Forgiveness", Dec. 12, 2013 https://www.youtube.com/watch?v=uptsIngNxCY

28. Quotes taken from The Daily Mail UK, "I Forgive You", June 19, 2015 https://www.dailymail.co.uk/news/article-3131874/Repent-Relatives-Charleston-killer-s-victims-confront-court-heart-wrenching-speeches-FORGIVENESS-adopts-vacant-remorseless-stare.html and People.com article "Gracious Relatives of Shooting Victims Offer Forgiveness", June 19, 2015 https://people.com/crime/gracious-relatives-of-shooting-victims-offer-forgiveness-for-accused-charleston-gunman-as-they-confront-him-in-court-hate-wont-win/

CHAPTER 7

29. Statistics verified by the Gun Violence Archive, July, 2021. https://www.gunviolencearchive.org/

30. From the article "2020 Was The Deadliest Gun Violence Year In Decades … ", The Washington Post, by Reis Thebault, Joe Fox and Andrew Ba Tran, June 14, 2021: https://www.washingtonpost.com/nation/2021/06/14/2021-gun-violence/?utm_campaign=wp_post_most&utm_medium=email&utm_source=newsletter&wpisrc=nl_

most&carta-url=https://s2.washingtonpost.com/car-ln-tr/339b774/60c7 84c29d2fdae3027dfe47/5f08d2d2ae7e8a4360bad9be/10/76/60c784c2 9d2fdae3027dfe47

31. For more on this see the article "While We're Talking About Guns In America … " by Rick Pidcock, July 19, 2021, Baptist News: https:// baptistnews.com/article/while-were-talking-about-guns-in-america-lets-talk-about-our-fear-based-theology-that-also-drives-gun-sales

32. Stephanie Coontz, in her book, *The Way We Never Were: American Families and the Nostalgia Trap* (New York: Basic Books, 1992), p. 184

33. Ronald A. Wells, History Through the Eyes of Faith (New York: HarperCollins Publishers, 1989), p. 179.

34. John D'Emilio and Estelle Freedman, *Intimate Matters: A History of Sexuality in America* (New York: Harper and Row, 1988), pp. 65, 133-134

35. https://www.brennancenter.org/our-work/analysis-opinion/ americas-faulty-perception-crime-rates

36. https://www.nytimes.com/2019/09/18/health/abortion-rate-dropped. html

37. From Arizona State University article: "Altheide says media driving discourse on fear": http://www.asu.edu/feature/includes/spring05/read-more/altheide.html

38. As quoted in my book Jesus Untangled: Crucifying Our Politics To Pledge Allegiance To The Lamb, pg. 111-112.

39. As quoted in Psychology Today Magazine, "If It Bleeds, It Leads", June 7, 2011, https://www.psy-chologytoday.com/blog/two-takes-depression/201106/ if-itbleeds-it-leads-understanding-fear-based-media

40. IBID

41. Taken from my book "Jesus Untangled: Crucifying Our Politics To Pledge Allegiance To The Lamb", pg. 113

42. From Benjamin L. Corey's blog post, The Potential Beauty That Could Come From Dying For An Enemy: https://www.benjaminlcorey.com/ the-potential-beauty-that-could-come-from-dying-for-an-enemy/

CHAPTER 8

43. Quoted from War: Four Christian Views, various authors, page. 145

44. From Tertullian's Apology, Chapter XXI. http://www.earlychristianwrit-ings.com/text/tertullian01.html

45. For further study, see the book "Constantine, the Great" by Michael Grant.

46. From my book Subversive Interviews: Volume 1, pg.62

47. IBID

48. IBID

49. From the interview with Grant Morrison in Vulture Magazine, Nov. 22, 2016: https://www.vulture.com/2016/11/grant-morrison-savage-sword-jesus-christ.html

50. IBID

51. *Myron S. Augsburger, from the book, War: Four Christian Views, page 93.*

52. From July 19, 2019 report "Strengthening the Military Family Readiness System for a Changing American Society." https://www.ncbi.nlm.nih.gov/books/NBK547615/

53. From a letter by Captain Robert Miles, King's Shropshire Light Infantry, who was attached to the Royal Irish Rifles, published in the Daily Mail and the Wellington Journal & Shrewsbury News in January 1915, following his death in action on 30 December 1914.

CHAPTER 9

54. From the NY Times article, "Midshipman, Then Pacifist: Rare Victory To Leave Navy" Feb. 23, 2001: https://www.nytimes.com/2011/02/23/nyregion/23objector.html?pagewanted=all&_r=1&

55. See Narcissistic Traits of Police Officers in America, Paloma Moran, San Jose State University: https://scholarworks.sjsu.edu/cgi/viewcontent.cgi?referer=https://www.google.com/&httpsredir=1&article=1049&context=themis#:~:text=Police%20officers%20with%20narcissistic%20traits,et%20al.%2C%202013

And https://scholarworks.sjsu.edu/themis/vol5/iss1/2/

56. In addition to the examples already shared previously in this book, see also these articles: "Armed Robber Flees Home After Women Chant the Name 'Jesus'" from The Christian Post, Jan. 28, 2013: https://www.christianpost.com/news/armed-robber-flees-home-after-women-chant-the-name-jesus.html

"Boy Released By Annoyed Kidnapper After Singing Gospel Song For 3 Hours", Review Journal, April 24, 2014: https://www.review-journal.com/uncategorized/boy-released-by-annoyed-kidnapper-after-singing-gospel-song-for-3-hours/#:~:text=2%3A09%20pm-,A%20 9%2Dyear%2Dold%20boy%20who%20was%20kidnapped%20-from%20his,in%20front%20of%20his%20homes.
"Woman's Jesus Talk Dissuades Would-Be Robber", WPBF 25 New, July 30, 2010: https://www.youtube.com/watch?v=UkkVWsP_q8w

"Woman Uses Holy Spirit To Shield Off A Robber", USCCA, Jan. 28, 2019: https://www.youtube.com/watch?v=fBXwnWGcf_k

57. From the article: "While We're Talking About Guns In America" by Rick Pidcock, July 19, 2021, Baptist News Global: https://baptistnews.com/article/while-were-talking-about-guns-in-america-lets-talk-about-our-fear-based-theology-that-also-drives-gun-sales/

CHAPTER 10

58. Tertullian, Apology; Appendix to Part 9

59. Tertullian, Apology, Chapter 30

60. Tertullian, The Chaplet or De Corona; chapter 11

61. IBID

62. Tertullian, Apology, Chapter 19

63. For Herb Montgomery's more complete and excellent research on this topic visit: https://renewedheartministries.com/Esights/09-05-2012

CHAPTER 11

64. From the book Mohandas Gandhi: Essential Writings, edited by John Dear, pg. 48

65. IBID, pg. 81

66. IBID, pg. 123

67. IBID, pg. 79

68. IBID, pg. 99

APPENDIX 3

69. From Dialogue with Trypho 110.3.4

70. From Protrepticus XI, 116

71. From "On Idolatry"

72. From Contra Celsius Book VII

73. From Divine Institutes IV

74. From Chapter 12 of Book 1

75. From Taitian's Address to the Greeks

76. From The First Apology of Justin Martyr

77. From The Apology of Aristides

78. From To the Ephesians

79. From Adversus Gentes I:VI

80. From A Plea for the Christians

81. From Homilies on the Beatitudes

82. From Origen, Contra Celsum, Book 3, Chapter 7

For more information about Keith Giles
or to contact him for speaking engagements,
please visit *www.KeithGiles.com*

Many voices. One message.

Quoir is a boutique publisher
with a singular message: *Christ is all.*
Venture beyond your boundaries to discover Christ
in ways you never thought possible.

For more information, please visit
www.quoir.com

HERETIC HAPPY HOUR

Burning questions, not people.

Heretic Happy Hour is an unapologetically irreverent, crass, and sometimes profound conversation about the Christian faith. Hosts, Keith Giles, Katy Valentine, Derrick Day, and Matthew Distefano pull no punches and leave no stones unturned. For some serious sacred cow-tipping, there's nothing better than spending an hour of your time with us.

www.heretichappyhour.com